The Secret Diary of

SIMON COWELL

The Secret Diary of SIMON COWELL

THE CHILDHOOD YEARS

by TONY COWELL

The author has pledged to donate a percentage of his royalties from the sale of this book to the Children's Hospice South West. A charity that provides hospice care for children with life limiting conditions.

JR
BOOKS

**The views and opinions expressed in the book
are entirely those of the author.**

Acknowledgements

My apologies to all members of my family who are not mentioned in this book, which is quite a lot actually; including Luke, Katie, Georgia, Harrison, John, June, Alex, Elizabeth, Jamie, Michael, Kathy, Penny, Malcolm and Auntie Elsie. But as you will soon discover, this book *may* be based on fact but it does contain a *huge* dollop of fiction! So I guess that's why Nicholas features rather a lot!

Special thanks to Emma for her extremely witty contributions and her patience during my many grumpy moments. And to Martin and Jan Lloyd for being there.

I remain indebted to The Mosaic Hotel, Biff and Toby at The Shed, and Steve at The Killigrew Inn.

To Jeremy Robson who believed so passionately in the idea from the start. My editor Lesley who turned corn syrup into fine wine. To Lisa Zibamanzar for her fantastic illustration – and to my mum Julie who was the original inspiration for this book. Her life has been transformed by my brother's celebrity and I honestly believe it is only a matter if time before she takes over from Oprah Winfrey.

And finally, I owe a huge debt to my brother Simon for bringing so much wit and creative entertainment into the world. I remain in awe of all the things he has achieved and eternally grateful for the way he continues to inspire me.

Tony Cowell

Introduction

I consider myself extremely fortunate to be the one to unearth one of the world's greatest texts. I'm not saying this diary is more significant than the Dead Sea scrolls or discovering Pompeii but it must rank as a very important find indeed. I say fortunate because I can only shudder at the thought of what may have happened had this diary fallen into the wrong hands. For when I embarked on my quest I knew from the very beginning I was not the only one who was aware of its existence, and for many years I have had to keep one step ahead of my deadly adversaries along the way.

As I entered the old house and climbed the stairs to the loft my heart began to race. The floor creaked beneath me as I fumbled my way down the long dark corridor using my torch. All the rooms were empty, their doors ajar, except for one room which lay at the end of the corridor. I shined my torch on the door and then I saw them: the three gold stars. I pushed the door with my shoulder and entered the cold damp room. As I slowly lifted the mattress a swarm of cockroaches crawled out over my hands and the tattered brown leather book slipped onto the floor at my feet. I anxiously fingered the yellowing pages and immediately recognized the handwriting. For me this was the end of a long and perilous journey. One that has taken me three decades and across two continents, following a mysterious set of clues and false tracks in a bid to unearth a hidden treasure that was hitherto thought lost forever.

Given the age of the manuscript it is reasonable to assume that some of the pages have gone missing, or have been destroyed over the years – so I have collated only those which are readable, and where necessary I have taken a little artistic licence to fill in the missing dates and events.

For this is a story of the boy who would be king. It all began one starry night, long, long ago...

On October 7th 1959 a strange bright light appeared over Brighton. A throng of celebrities and music mystics had made the long journey on camels from far-flung places to witness the birth of the special child his mother had already dubbed 'The Nasty One'.

Boy, is this baby different or what?

'So what shall we call him?' asked mum.

'How about Damien?' said dad.

'No,' said mum. 'This boy is special; he shall be called...Simon.'

The world held its breath.

Some years later Simon discovered The Guinness Book of Hit Singles *and he had a revelation: he was going to conquer the world, to make music beautiful, and to search the land for top talent that would make the people happy again. Oh, and to make television shows that were about real people and not just Daleks.*

The world breathed again.

November 7th 1966

I am seven years old and live in a beautiful big house in a town called Helstree. I live with my mum and dad, my younger brother Nicholas (who is much smaller than me) and my big brother Tony. Nanny Heather looks after us when mum's not here — which is all the time because she spends most days in the garden collecting bugs.

I have a cat called Archie, a dog called Bwana and a whole five acres of garden. Oh...and we have a gardener called Mr Biggers — who spends a lot of time in the potting shed on his own. Dad says Mr Biggers is a wizard and makes magic potions in the shed.

Over the fence next door, a short tractor ride away, lives Uncle Gerry. Uncle Gerry does things with film stars and is boss of a great big film studio. Last week a lady with long dark hair called Liz came to stay with him. I know she's a film star because she has a very loud voice and drinks a lot. She's making a film called Cleopatra with a man from Wales called Richard who has funny holes in his face. Mum goes over the fence every afternoon for drinks. In fact, I don't know why she doesn't move next door and take her jars of bugs with her.

As I look out of my window all I can see is grass and trees — when I grow up I want to buy a big house like this — but without the silly gold bits. The sun is shining all over the garden and the only bad thing about today is I have to go to school. I hate it. But mum says I won't make any money unless I'm good at school. And when I'm older she says I will have to go to university because nobody makes any money unless they go there. I think she is lying because she made lots of money by dancing on a stage with feathers on her head.

I've decided to write a diary so I can remember all the horrible things that have happened to me. When I was two years old mum made Tony take me out in my pink pram. He pushed me so fast he lost control and hit the wall of Mrs Radcliffe's sweet shop and I bashed my head on the Walls Ice cream sign. I can still feel the bump today and I'm worried it might affect me when I grow up.

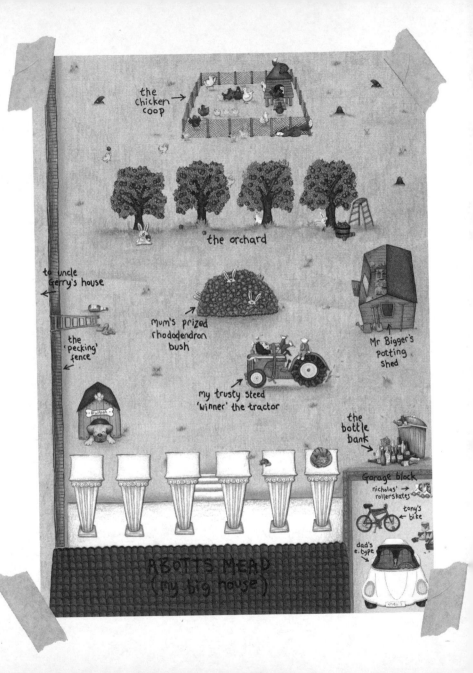

NOTE TO SELF:

AS CHRISTMAS IS COMING I'M GOING TO WRITE
MY NEW YEAR'S RESOLUTIONS:

- I WILL WEAR MY TROUSERS THE WAY I WANT
TO.

- I WILL SMOKE WHEN I GROW UP.

- I WILL ALWAYS BE NICE TO PEOPLE WHEN I
GROW UP (UNLESS THEY ARE REALLY USELESS).

- I WON'T WATCH TV ANYMORE BECAUSE ALL
THE PEOPLE ON THERE ARE REALLY SILLY.

- I WILL MAKE SURE NICHOLAS IS ALWAYS
SMALLER THAN ME.

8th November 1966

— Awful day

Felt rotten. It was mother's fault for singing Fly Me to the Moon at 2am at the top of the stairs with Uncle Gerry from next door. I never want to hear that song again. I'm allergic to it. The spot on my chin has got bigger — it's mother's fault for not knowing about vitamins — it's a miracle we don't all have scurvy. Next year I could be in a children's home for sure. When I grow up I'm going to use loads of vitamins, face creams, and put tomatoes in my bath to keep my skin young.

School is a waste of time. I think I'm different from all the other kids. I'm not saying I'm special — just different. No, actually, on second thoughts, I think I am special.

Today I have a music lesson. And I hate music — I

think it's horrible. Mrs Scofield always makes us sing.
It's all such a terrible noise. I hate singers. Big brother
Tony keeps playing a record by a man with scary hair
called Bob Dylan who sounds like our cat Archie, but
worse. A singing poet? It just bored me to tears. He
plays it over and over again. He says it's groovy,
whatever that means. Mum says it's just a phase he's
going through — well, I only hope it doesn't last too
long.

November 9th 1966

— Clever me

I had an idea of how to get out of school today. I put
my face on the radiator for five minutes until it was
really red and hot. Then I jumped back into bed and
shouted for dad to come up.

He came in the room and took one look at me and said, 'What's the matter son, you look terrible?'

'I'm really hot, dad — feel my forehead.' He put his hand on my head and quickly removed it. 'You've got a temperature son — you stay in bed. I'll phone the school.'

Once you know how to get round your parents, you never look back. Mum, of course, will always be a pain — but as long as I get to dad first I always get my own way.

I had a good lie-in till 11am and then went downstairs to the kitchen. Mum was dressed in one of her bug hunting outfits, including a funny hat that made her look like a scarecrow. Mrs Hustler (our so-called cleaner) was at the sink humming. I don't like Mrs Hustler because she listens in to all mum's phone calls — which must be a full-time job.

'Feeling better already?' said mum, with a note of sarcasm.

'I don't feel that good,' I said, holding a hand to my head. 'But maybe a bit of fresh air would help.'

'If you don't feel well then you need to stay in bed. Or if it's fresh air you want, you can go to school.'

Nice try mum.

'Dad said I could get up if I felt better — and he said I should eat breakfast and just play quietly or watch television.'

'You can read a book then,' says mum. 'Watching television didn't do anyone any good. Television is for lazy people with no ambition. You read a book and learn something.'

'Mum?'

'Yes'

'Is it true that when I was born dad wanted to call me Damien?'

'Yes...'

November 10th 1966

— Must make more money

Another bad night. Tony came home late with a 'friend'. All I could hear was giggling and that terrible Bob Dylan noise again. I'm going to have to scratch that record really badly. And he's smoking something that stinks like old socks and I think it's giving me spots.

Dad didn't go to work today because he's got the flu. I'm not surprised with the diet we get. Thought about all those singers like The Beatles and Frank Sinatra. They make loads of records, and mum and Tony go out and buy them. They must make millions! But the people who make all the plastic records must make millions too. I might ask Uncle Gerry about it because Dad says Uncle Gerry is a know-all — and he's got a Rolls-Royce!

Mum says she has to get ready for Christmas soon and has too much to do. I don't think she does much at all because Mrs Hustler does all the cleaning, Nanny Heather does the cooking and mum is always on the phone. Then a big green van arrives and delivers all the food. When she's not over the fence dancing with the stars, she's putting pins through moths and reading the *National Geographic* magazine. I think mum should do more house work.

My Auntie Joan came round after school and was disgusted with the state of the house. I showed her my room, which is always neat and tidy, and she gave me two shillings. I showed her all the empty wine bottles in the dustbin and she was shocked and gave me another two shillings. (I think I'm going to do this more often.) She asked me what I wanted for Christmas and I told her an Oscar. She said you had to be an actor before you got an Oscar. I said in that case I'll think again. She also told me she knitted mum a woolly jumper every Christmas and mum had never worn any of them. I'm not surprised, they're all so ghastly.

Uncle Gerry came round for dinner with some chap called Roger Moore, who lives up the road. Mum always gets dressed up when Roger comes — I don't know why — it's not like he's famous or anything. Anyway, dad appears to be over his flu — maybe that Gordon's gin stuff is some sort of medicine. I made a fuss of Uncle Gerry and asked him how much money singers made.

'Singers?' he said.

'Yes,' I said.

'Well it depends who you mean. The Beatles are already millionaires. Everyone loves them.'

'Well I'm no judge,' I said, 'but I think they're crap.'

'Do you want to be a singer when you grow up Simon?' he asked.

'Not if I sound like Bob Dylan...'

My favourite song at the moment is *Unchained Melody* by a group called The Righteous Brothers. Now that's what I call music.

November 11th 1966

I've just watched a really silly programme on the television called **Juke Box Jury**. What do the folk on Telly know about pop music? I think television programmes like this should be banned. The thing is, I don't trust what other people say. In fact, I'm going to write to ask if I can be a judge on the show or maybe I'll wait till I'm a bit older...and taller, and my teeth have grown.

December 15th 1966
– My family

Mum says we all have to dress up for Christmas. She says we have to dress as our favourite film star. Dad has decided to dress up as that man in **My Fair Lady** and mum is going as Mary Poppins. Is it any wonder I want to leave home? And to top it all she has bought Nicholas and me matching blue velvet suits and white socks. Yuk! Can you believe it? There's no way I'm wearing that — she can get stuffed!

I've got no choice but to either start an accidental fire and burn the bloody suits or get Bwana the dog to rip the suits up in some sort of doggy fit — he's already practised on the postman. And I thought Christmas was a time of fun and presents — not for dressing up and making a complete fool of yourself. I blame Uncle Gerry and all his actor friends.

I've made a decision. I'm going to set light to the velvet suits in the attic and get Nicholas to help me.

While mum was out collecting bugs again I grabbed Nicholas out of his playroom (he was lying on top of his Rupert Bear). I snatched the two suits from mum's bedroom and climbed the ladder to the loft. And guess what? Hidden at the back of the loft I found dad's

Santa Claus outfit — the one he wears every Christmas when he creeps into our room with our presents. The thing is, I know that Santa doesn't exist — but Nicholas doesn't. What a dumbo! So I took great pleasure in pulling out the Santa suit and stamping on it in front of him.

'Is Santa dead, he looks so thin?' asked Nicholas in a whiny voice.

'Don't be an idiot!' I snapped. 'He was never alive — and we're going to burn him, so get ready to dance round the fire.'

'No don't!' cried Nicholas.

'Why not?'

'Because then he won't be able to bring us any presents on Christmas day.'

'Oh shut up Nicholas — dad brings your presents — not Santa bloody Claus.'

I kicked Nicholas out of the way, took a box of matches from my pocket and then chucked the velvet suits on top of Santa. I lit a match and grinned at Nicholas's wide-eyed look of horror. Very soon thick black smoke began to fill the room and I almost began to panic.

Brother Tony, who was supposed to be keeping an eye on us, smelled the burning and came running up the stairs in that mad panic that only Tony does so well. He quickly put the fire out and was able to somehow salvage Santa's body, but sadly not his legs — or the bloody velvet suits. THANK GOD!

I can't wait for Christmas day...

NOTE TO SELF:
NEVER BELIEVE A SINGLE WORD YOUR PARENTS TELL YOU.

December 20th 1966

Uncle Gerry had a birthday party next door for his silly daughter called Tessa and mum said Nicholas and I had to go. What a waste of time watching girls play with dolls houses. But Nicholas seemed to enjoy it.

I met another one of those film people called Bette Davis and she's got very strange eyes. She made me sit on her lap which was really big and squidgy. Then she blew smoke all over me and asked me if I wanted to be an actor when I grow up. I said no because all actors smell. Then she put me down with a thump and told me to go play in the garden. I don't like actors because they get loads of money for pretending to be someone else. And that's not fair!

December 21st 1966
— Nicholas gets the chop

Nicholas is such a willing apprentice I've made him chief test pilot for all my new schemes. Today I decided he needed a haircut for Christmas — and I would be the one who would give it to him.

I snatched his Rupert Bear off him and sat him on a stool, tied his arms and legs, and pulled out a huge pair of scissors from mum's sewing basket and chopped off several large chunks of his hair. I thought I'd better stop when he began to look like a mad monk with his scalp peeking through the top.

Once I had finished the job, I gave him back his Rupert Bear and told him to go and show his new style to mum. All I could hear was mum's terrible screechy voice as it wailed through the house: *Who the bloody hell did that to you?'*

I have now come to the conclusion that people don't really appreciate my creative side.

December 25th 1966
— Santa's dead

Dad finally announced that he will never dress up as Father Christmas ever again. Good. What was the bloody point anyway — I'm so delighted.

I'm even more delighted that Nicholas has been crying all morning and I'm to blame, of course, for telling him the truth about Santa. I'm sooooooo happy. It's the best Christmas day ever!

I don't mean to be nasty...but, I always think it's best to tell people the truth. What's the point in lying to them? Just tell them the way it is — that's going to be my life motto.

Auntie Joan came round for Christmas lunch and I couldn't wait for mum to open Auntie's present. And guess what? Another ghastly woolly jumper. This time Auntie insisted that mum put it on straight away. I was in fits as mum came into the room wearing a bright yellow cardigan with all the signs of the zodiac down the back. Hideous, but at least I got what I wanted — a brand new Captain Scarlet outfit.

I will remember this Christmas as the year I finally grew up. I'd been measuring myself every day for six months. I'd noticed that a lot of kids at school had shot up and overtaken me. Mum (sounding all Fanny Cradock-like) said it was all to do with what you eat. Easy for her to say as it was hard to find any food in our house apart from cheese balls and twiglets. So for the last three months I've been upping my levels of baked beans and custard creams, and this morning I discovered I'd grown an inch in three months. I worked out that by the time I'm 14 I'll be six foot nine inches and won't need to wear those Cuban heels that Tony wears. Well. I hope not anyway...

December 26th 1966

I've been wearing my Captain Scarlet outfit all day. I think brother Tony might be a Mysteron. His voice sounds the same so I'm keeping very clear of him. Nicholas is very jealous of my outfit but I think he really likes dolls.

February 12th 1967

— I thought mums were supposed to cook...

Mum's been experimenting in the kitchen again. She's made something called a cheese fondue. It looks like dog sick. Why on earth she feels she has to make food like this I'll never know. If I don't get proper food soon I'm never going to grow properly and I'll end up short and stumpy.

THE WORST THINGS MUM MAKES FOR DINNER:

- Braised steak
- Cheese fondue
- Tripe and onions (forgot what tripe is but it's not good)
- Potted meat (what IS that?)
- Pigs' trotters — I mean, eating the poor pig's feet, that's horrible

February 13th 1967

There are these twins at school called the
McDougals. They both have big heads and red hair.
They keep calling me *Scowell*. They pushed me up
against the wall today and said my trousers were too
high and I'd never get any girls. I told them to mind
their own business and I will have as many girls as I
like when I'm older. Tomorrow I'm taking my Captain
Scarlet gun to school.

February 14th 1967
— Days that should be banned

Today is what they call Valentine's Day. Who the
bloody hell thought this up? The whole house is pink
— it's appalling. I can't think of anything worse than
buying flowers or chocolates and having to hand

I AM CAPTAIN SCARLET

them over to someone else — what a waste. Mum says it's a way of expressing your love for your partner. Yeah, right! But guess what? Nanny Heather made Nicholas write a poem to mum and it's so hilariously bad I've decide to rip it up before she can read it. Now that's what I call real love...

> My mom is very sweet and cool...
> She worries bout me when I am in school.
> She makes sure that I get there on time
> So that I don't feel like a fool.
>
> Love Nicholas

YUK!!!

February 16th 1967

— My first tipple

It was dad's birthday today and he had one of his silly noisy parties last night with all that Perry Como music. It was like the outpatient's of an insane asylum. I think mum was a bit tipsy because she showed me all her boring *National Geographic* magazines. The good news was dad let Nicholas and me have our very first drink. The bad news was it was sherry and tasted like cough medicine.

Sherry stinks!

February 17th 1967

— My first and last hangover!

Today I have a headache — it's official — and it's dad's fault for making me drink that sherry. How can parents be so irresponsible? I'm definitely not going to be a parent when I grow up. And to make things worse, Tony's got a new record by a bloke called Jimi Hendrix. It's like a loud screechy guitar that goes on and on and right through my head. I hate guitars. Growing up in this house is definitely not suitable for young children. I think I might go and live in the chicken coop.

February 18th 1967

IF I EVER BECOME PRIME MINISTER THESE ARE THE FIRST TV SHOWS I WILL BAN:

- Thank Your Lucky Stars
- Ready Steady Go!
- Top of the Pops
- This Is Your Life

March 7th 1967

It was Nicholas's birthday today. I hate other people's birthdays because I don't get any presents. To make things worse Nicholas had a party and invited Tessa from next door and all her silly friends. The parents wanted us to dress up and put on a show and everyone got some sweets. So Nicholas dressed up as Rupert Bear and I put on my Captain Scarlet outfit. Then this really grumpy girl called Karen with red hair and spots on her chin said she wasn't going to do the show unless she got more sweets than anyone else.

'But you've already had three packets of love hearts you greedy git,' I said.

Then she gave me this really scary look and said:

'Well I'm not going to be in the show unless I get two Crunchies and some Rolos.'

I told her I didn't think that was fair and she stormed downstairs and told her mum I was really mean. You know what? I think girls are very confusing.

March 12th 1967

— people who work in TV are very silly

Mum says dad shouldn't watch so much television because it's making him fat. He loves this programme called *The Prisoner*. It's about a man who is kidnapped and kept in a mysterious village which looks like a Butlin's holiday camp except it's guarded by giant white balls that come out of houses to stop him running away. Grown-ups are very weird. I think television is rubbish and all the people who work in it are very silly.

MY FAVOURITE CARTOON CHARACTERS:

- Jinx The Cat
- Popeye
- The Flinstones
- Yogi Bear
- The Pink Panther

March 13th 1967

— Telling people the truth

My diary is my secret place where I can say what I like. I like telling people what I really think about them. I can tell them when they look awful or they speak funny. I think this is going to be my job. So here goes... Nicholas's voice is much higher than mine and he sounds like a girl. Mum wears clothes that make her look like a scarecrow and Nanny Heather wears her skirts too short **and** she's got a boyfriend who waits down by the front gate and I've seen them kiss. Yuk!!

March 15th 1967

— Doing well at school

I hate school dinners; they are worse than mum's. Today we had mince and mashed potato and the mash tasted like cardboard so I tipped it all onto Teddy Johnson's plate and he started to cry. Then a little girl tipped her glass of water all over Teddy's head and told him to shut up. Then she grabbed my glass of water and threw it over his head too. Mrs Scofield came running over and sent her to the headmaster's office and told me how good I was for being the first to finish my dinner.

Result!....

March 21st 1967

I don't like Harold Wilson he's a dope. I don't think he knows how to run a country. Dad says we would be much better off if we had another man in charge. I think he said his name is Mr Tory. I don't know why *dad* isn't prime minister — he seems to know it all anyway.

March 22nd 1967

I hate all this 'flower power' rubbish. I think it's silly. Brother Tony has flowers in his hair and now Nanny Heather has started playing this Radio 1 thing all day. What a racket. I prefer dad's Frank Sinatra records, at least you can hear what he's singing about. I can't understand a word that the Rolling Stones sing — *and* they dress like tramps.

March 23rd 1967

I need to find a way to make more pocket money. I want a big wallet like dad's with loads of paper money in it. Why mum only gives us change I'll never know — it doesn't last very long at all. I want to make loads of paper money when I'm older because I reckon it lasts longer. When I grow up I'm going to be rich and then tell everyone what to do.

April 12th 1967

Bwana the dog ate the postman this morning and dad went mad. Now Bwana has to live in a kennel in the garden and he's tied up. Mr Biggers says he's very scared of Bwana and that sometimes he tries to bite his bottom if he bends down. I'm not sure that Dad's right about Mr Biggers being a Wizard. I think he's just a fake with a rake.

April 15th 1967

I've just worked out what that Roger Moore bloke does. He's in that Saint thing on TV. And guess what? Mum's now got the same car as Roger — it's a white Volvo. I think she's just a show-off. When I'm old enough to drive I'm going to have an Aston Martin like James Bond. Nicholas should get a mini because he's so small.

April 17th 1967

I just heard Mum telling Dad that she wants to go to Africa to search for bugs. She's mad about collecting bugs and wants to be famous and on the telly like that David Attenborough. I think she should just learn to cook properly and spend the whole day cleaning. Dad says that's what mums are meant to do. I really hope she doesn't go on television. I won't allow anyone in our family to go on there!

April 18th 1967

Here is my list of things I'm going to do when I'm really rich — and they are very important:

• BUILD TONY A REALLY COMFORTABLE PADDED CELL WITH A LOCK ON IT SO THAT NOBODY (ESPECIALLY ME) CAN HEAR ANY OF HIS TERRIBLE RECORDS.

• BUY SOME SORT OF FUNNY DRINK I CAN GIVE TO MUM TO STOP HER TALKING.

• BUY NICHOLAS HIS OWN ROOM SO HE DOESN'T HAVE TO KEEP BRINGING HIS RUPERT BEAR INTO MY ROOM TO PLAY WITH.

• BUY A FAST CAR SO I CAN GET AWAY FROM HERE VERY QUICKLY.

April 19th 1967

Mum says brother Tony wants to be an actor and he's going to stage school. I think mum doesn't want him to go there because she thinks acting is really hard unless you are a great actor like Errol Flynn or Liz Taylor.

I think Tony would be great playing that man Rasputin — because he has long hair, a big moustache and mad eyes.

May 6th 1967
— Mum's beginning to bug me

Mum says that I'm falling behind in school and I need to try harder. She's taken away all my Superman comics and given me an encyclopaedia.

She says I have to start learning about the real world now.

'What do you know about insects Simon?' she said.

'Nothing at all mum'

'Did you know that the female Madagascar hissing cockroach carry their eggs (and neonatal nymphs) inside their bodies?'

'No mum — I didn't.'

How useful — NOT!

May 7th 1967

This morning Nanny Heather took me down to the shops to buy T-shirts. She chose a bright pink one which was awful so I said I wanted a black one. I think black looks best on me. So she bought them both and gave Nicholas the pink one. Hah!

May 14th 1967

There was yet another party at home tonight. I think
the whole of bloody Hollywood was there. All I could
hear was girls trying to sing along to a Petula Clark
song. Dreadful! I wish people didn't try to sing if they
sound like cats. Someone needs to tell them. 'You have
just invented a new form of torture!' I shouted down
the stairs. Nobody heard my cry for help.

May 21st 1967

I just caught Nicholas in front of the TV singing along
to the Milky Bar Kid advert. I have heard some bad
performances in my time. And I can honestly say that
this is one of the worst of them. Mum says he now
wants a cowboy outfit so he can wear it to school.
That's never going to happen — and I can just imagine
what the McDougal twins would say if he did...

June 5th 1967

Mum and dad went to a garden party at Uncle Gerry's tonight. Mum came down the stairs wearing a bright yellow dress and matching hat.

'Does mummy look pretty?' she asked, twirling around the hall.

'No,' I said. 'You look like a canary' — and ran into the kitchen laughing.

Then I heard the front door slam.

Good riddance that's what I say. Now I'm going to get my scalextric out. I'm going to be a faster driver than that Graham Hill when I grow up but without that silly moustache.

August 17th 1967

Now that it's summer I'm very worried about all the insects and small animals that may get killed in the garden. So I'm going to send a note to our gardener Mr Biggers:

Dear Mr Biggers

Please can you be very careful when you are digging in the garden so you don't kill any spiders or ants because I don't think anybody should be killed in the garden. But if you do find Bob Dylan in the garden I don't mind if he's made very dead indeed.

Thank you

Love Simon

September 17th 1967

I've been thinking about my future because I want to leave school as soon as possible because it's so bloody useless. I need to know how I'm going to make my money. Uncle Gerry makes money out of film stars. But I don't know what he does with them — but he has got a Rolls Royce and that's important. Dad sells houses and stuff but I think that's boring and the sort of thing Nicholas would do. And anyway where's the money in that?

September 28th 1967

It's my birthday next month so I thought I'd better make a list of things I want and then leave in every room in the house — which means I have to write it out twenty two times.

- THE MONKEES NEW LP

- ASTON MARTIN DB5

- THE JAMES BOND ATTACHE CASE

- FUZZY FELT POP STARS

- LEGO.

October 1st 1967

I've just been watching that Fireball XL5 on television.
It's so rubbish because you can see all the strings move
the puppets. How come? Why can't they paint the
strings a different colour so they blend into the
background? I could make a better TV show. So I got
a big cardboard box and made a TV set and put in
action man and pretended he was singing. Hmmmm...
what else... Then he shoots everybody.

October 7th 1967

Today is my birthday and I am eight. The only
presents I got from my list was the Aston Martin and
the Monkees new LP; which Tony let me play on his
Dansette Junior. Nicholas keeps trying to steal my
Aston Martin so I have hidden it in the breadbin in
the kitchen. In the meantime I have to put up with
all this children's party nonsense and Nicholas's silly
friends. I don't think mum knows where the kitchen
is so Nanny Heather has made all the sandwiches and
they're much better — but some of them have
avocado pear in them and they taste like green
slime.

October 8th 1967

Mum's favourite TV programme is *Life in the
Animal World* with a man called Desmond Morris

who hasn't got any hair. Dad says he looks like a monkey but mum says he's very cuddly and speaks very quietly (not like her!). I prefer *Animal Magic* because Johnny Morris makes real animals talk. Dad likes *The Avengers* and Nicholas watches *The Railway Children* because he says he loves Jenny Agutter. Yuk!

October 12th 1967

I don't think mum knows how to wash up dishes because she always gets Nanny Heather to do it. Mum says that in America they have machines to do it and wants Dad to buy her one. Dad says they don't work properly and they will make women even more lazy than they are already.

November 5th 1967

It's bonfire night tonight and mum's made what she calls firework soup and strangely it does taste quite nice which makes a change from most of the things she cooks. I'm not sure I like fireworks and Bwana hates them; he puts his paws over his ears so he can't hear the bangs. I think I might tie up Nicholas and Rupert Bear and stick them on top of the bonfire. Then see if Tony can rescue them in time.

December 12th 1967
— Getting ready for Christmas.

Now that Santa's dead, this Christmas will be the best so far. I can't wait to see dad bringing my presents into my bedroom without that silly Santa suit on. Hah!

Nicholas has been crying again because he says all his friends at school believe in Father Christmas and he doesn't know how to tell them he's not real. So I said I was more than happy to break the news to them if that helps. Besides, there's no point in letting kids believe in something that's not real. It's always best to tell people the truth I reckon.

FOR CHRISTMAS I WANT:

- STAR TREK OUTFIT WITH V-NECK IN BLACK

- WATER PISTOL

- A NICE DESK AND CHAIR

- THUNDERBIRDS ROCKET

- MORE MARBLES

December 13th 1967

— My first Nativity

Guess what — now I've been banned from the school orchestra. Mrs Scofield gave me the coconuts to play in the school nativity play. What?!

'COWELL!' — shouts Mrs Scofield.

'Slow that donkey down right now! Try for a gentle plod in time with the rest of the orchestra.'

'Look Miss,' I said. 'If the donkey got a bloody move on Mary would get there a damn sight sooner and the Innkeeper may still have some rooms free.'

Then she told the whole class I was a nuisance and shouldn't try and rewrite the birth of Christ. Now I have to just sit there and watch...SO BORING!! Joseph's singing is appalling — he looks good, but his voice is distinctly average.

December 15th 1967

— Telling Auntie Joan the truth

This morning I told mum I don't want people dressing up this Christmas and can we all be normal. I also told Auntie Joan NOT to knit mum anymore crappy jumpers because mum has given all the ones she gave her to the charity shop. Auntie Joan looked quite shocked and sad — but, if I'm being honest, I feel it's my duty to tell people the facts — even though sometimes they hurt. Hah!

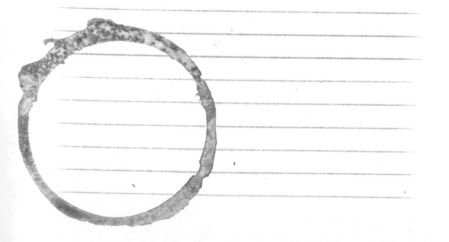

December 17th 1967

— My car collection

Now I've got my Aston Martin I've decided I want a whole collection of fast cars. So this Christmas I'm going to make sure everyone buys me one. I think cars are very important to boys. When I grow up I'm going to spend all my money on fast cars — just like dad and Uncle Gerry. Even brother Tony has just got his first real car but it's crap. It's an old grey minivan with doors on the back and no windows. Mum says he's got blankets in there too. God only knows what he does in there!

December 25th 1967

— It's Christmas day!

I just had to stay awake last night so I could catch dad coming into my bedroom with my presents.

So I put six saucepans and two frying pans on top of my door so when he tried to creep in my room at midnight they all fell on top of him with a big clatter. I don't think Dad found it very funny but I could hear mum giggling down the hall.

At 11am on Christmas day Auntie Joan came round and before I let her in, I made sure she didn't have any funny jumpers with her. Then we had brunch which is when dad eats kippers and mum drinks champagne. Then Uncle Gerry and that Roger Moore bloke came round and mum gave everyone a present and the talking seemed to get louder.

Then Nicholas came downstairs and threw his Rupert Bear at me and started crying. He said that Christmas will never be the same again because Santa Claus was dead. Mum wiped his eyes and said that, in a way, I was right to tell him that Father Christmas didn't exist and that the world would be a better place if everyone told the truth like me. So, for the first time in her life I think mum said the right thing. I so like being RIGHT!

Happy Christmas Diary!

February 12th 1968

— Back to school and more trouble

Mrs Scofield made me stand outside the headmaster's office today. I don't have a watch but I reckon I was there at least fourteen hours. I was supposed to stay there until I realised how rude and naughty I was. But how would I know when I've realised? I stand by what I said. **Frère Jacques** is a ghastly tune and not even British. I see little point in learning the words to something, and then play it on the recorder.

Mrs Schofield says I'm naturally deaf to the joy of music. What does she know?

I hate school.

February 13th 1968

— I know how to decorate better than mum

Mother announced this morning that she plans to redecorate the whole top floor which of course includes my bedroom. She asked if I had any ideas about what I'd like to have on my walls. I said that I had loads of ideas. I saw it as a great chance for me to get rid of all that horrid gold flowery rubbish and turn it into a proper boy's room!

'What about white?' I said. 'But with a painting of a black Aston Martin on the wall. And wouldn't it be cool if my bed was actually in the shape of a car?'

Dad said that if I wanted to sleep in a car there were several in the garage that I could use. I don't think dad understands.

February 15th 1968

Tony is really moody. He spends hours sitting in the orchard writing love poems in a notebook. He's so weird. When I went up to him to ask him if he was writing a diary like mine, he said that I wouldn't understand and I was just a baby.

Then he said that he'd already read my diary anyway and it was full of rubbish and I wouldn't know the first thing about being deep. Deep? Who wants to be deep? Holes are deep, ponds are deep but why would a person want to be deep? You could drown and that would be very bad. I'm now going to hide my diary in a much better place. So, if you're reading this now Tony, I think your arms are hairy and nobody will ever want to kiss you. Ha!

March 1st 1968

It's Saturday and no school today hooray! We're going up to London and I am so excited. Mum says we're going to buy special clothes for a special day.

That posh lady from church, Dame Edith Shatwell, is having a garden party. Mum says we have to be on our best behaviour or we'll never be allowed out in 'Polite Society' again. I don't know where Polite Society is, but I think it's near our house.

So we're off to the big green shop which is mum's favourite. But we always have to hide the green bags when we get home so Dad doesn't see how many things Mum has bought.

March 8th 1968

— Today is Tony's 18th birthday

Blimey he so old already! Mum bought Tony a ghastly velvet jacket and says he looks like George Harrison. I think he looks more like Cliff Richard, YUK! Dad bought him two wing mirrors for his minivan because he insists Tony keeps hitting the garage wall when he comes home late at night.

I didn't buy him anything because he keeps me awake every night with all his silly music. Mum says Tony's having a party tonight in his room. In that case, I said, I'm definitely going to sleep in the chicken coop.

March 20th 1968

I'm devastated. Mum has bought more matching outfits for me and Nicholas. We look like fluffy versions of Benny, the blue one from *Top Cat* — except not as chubby.

First it was going to be brown corduroy, and then she settled on blue. I said I wanted black but mum said I was in no position to judge fashion, given that I had cut the arms off of my best green suit jacket. (Green is so shit!)

She told me to remember how lucky I was to have clothes at all — as there were some people in the world who didn't even have a vest. (I think she means Mr Biggers!)

May 2nd 1968

— Nicholas's fête

I think it is disgraceful that mum and
dad carried on after me and made Nicholas.

If I'm being honest I think Nicholas was a back—up
plan in case I turned out to be strange or ugly. So now
I wonder if they'd mind if I tried to sell him at the
village fête.

I told mum that I wanted to raise money for dogs and
have my own stall at the village fête.

She looked at me and almost cried with pride.

'What a lovely boy you are,' she said, wiping her eyes
with a tea towel.

'But you're not old enough to go on your own and I've
got the hairdresser and my toenail lady coming so

Nanny Heather will have to take you.'

So we've been making cakes to sell ever since!
Nicholas couldn't wait to get involved. He put worms
in my fairy cake mixture. I didn't notice until some of
them started to make a bid for freedom up the side of
the bowl. Nanny Heather screamed when she saw
them — and she thought I did it and said I was wicked.
Now I'm definitely going to sell Nicholas for two
shillings at the fête.

May 5th 1968
— Cowboys in the garden

I was messing around in the garden playing cowboys
and Indians with Nicholas. I persuaded him that it was
my turn to capture him and so I found some rope in
the shed and tied him to the sit-on lawnmower.
Nicholas was soon firmly strapped to the seat, lying on
his back facing the sky. As luck would have it, the

keys were in the ignition, making the game more realistic as the machine magically became my horse — my trusty steed called **Winner**.

I started it up and off he went. He was squealing and shouting as I watched him head off towards the orchard. At that very moment I heard Nanny Heather saying she was serving cake and tea. So I ran off and began to tuck in to the cakes.

An hour later Nicholas was discovered in a large rhododendron bush. He wouldn't have been found at all if Bwana hadn't barked so loud. Then I heard mother shriek from the other side of the house. Have I killed him? Nah. Just ruined mother's prized shrub display that she invites Liz Taylor to admire.

I think I'm in giant trouble.

June 1st 1968

Dad went to get his Piccalilli out of the fridge and instead nearly scooped a spoonful of dead caterpillars onto his cheese sandwich. He went mad and told mum not to store her bugs in his Piccalilli or Branston jars. 'Keep them in the bloody potting shed,' he shouted.

But Mr Biggers said that wasn't a good idea because he's got tomato plants growing in there. So mum's gone off in a rage and taken them over to Uncle Gerry's house. I hope she puts them in Bette Davis's room.

June 5th 1969

I think I'm going to have to get mum one of those

fashion stylists. She's taken this 'summer of love' thing way too seriously — all long flowing dresses and beads — she looks like she's wearing somebody's curtains. Presumably her dressing room mirror is broken. She needs to get a grip because I'm not going anywhere in the car with her dressed like that. In fact, I think it's time I learned to drive myself. I want my own sports car like dad's. But more than one — maybe two or three of them. Mum should get a bike like Tony's.

July 6th 1969

It's 10.30pm and was just going to bed when I found Nicholas's Rupert Bear hidden under my bed so I've written Nicholas a note and pinned Rupert to his bedroom door with a drawing pin through his ear.

DEAR NICHOLAS,

IF YOU MUST PLAY WITH RUPERT BEAR — PLEASE
PLAY WITH IT IN YOUR OWN BEDROOM — NOT
IN MINE. UNLESS YOU REALLY WANT RUPERT TO
END UP LIKE DAD'S SANTA'S SUIT!!

IF I'M BEING HONEST, PERHAPS NOW IS A GOOD
TIME TO GET RID OF RUPERT ALTOGETHER AND
GET A TRAIN SET OR SOME MECCANO. THESE
ARE WHAT ARE CONSIDERED TO BE PROPER
TOYS FOR BOYS!

SIMON

July 7th 1969

— Tony in the chicken coop...

There was a lot of noise coming from the chicken coop at the bottom of the garden last night — and it wasn't the chickens. Mum said dad caught Tony in there smoking something he shouldn't have been. Anyway, dad said the chickens aren't very well now and their eggs will taste funny.

The good news is that Tony's gone to a pop concert in a place called the Island of White. He crept out the door really early this morning, which was a good job because if mum had seen him she'd have had a fit. He was wearing a long brown velvet coat with pink beads around his neck. What a weirdo!

I just don't get this whole music thing at the moment. Mick Jagger can't sing. The Who make such a racket. But I do like that new song called Sugar, Sugar.

July 8th 1969

IF I EVER GET ANY POCKET MONEY THIS IS WHAT
I NEED TO BUY:

- A BIGGER PAIR OF SCISSORS.

- ROPE TO TIE UP NICHOLAS.

- BLACK CLOTHES

- A DALEK

July 20th 1969

Mum and dad let us watch television tonight so we
could see the American spacemen land on the moon.
Afterwards Nicholas said he wanted to go and live on
the moon but mum said Rupert Bear won't be able to
breathe up there so he changed his mind. I think it

might be a better idea if Tony went to live up there.
Because in space, no one can hear Dylan scream.

August 16th 1969

— Mum goes over the 'Pecking Fence'

Uncle Gerry phoned this morning and invited mum for
drinks with an American actor called Gregory Peck,
whoever he is. No sooner had she put the phone
down than she dashed into her dressing room to get
changed. 'The dinner's in the oven — and I'll be back
in half an hour,' she yelled and skipped down the
driveway, swinging her skirt round.

About four hours later dad and I were in the garden
when we heard mum's tinny voice singing: 'The hills
are alive with the sound of music.' All of a sudden
her head appeared over the fence as Uncle Gerry and
this fellow Gregory Peck, with one hand under each
buttock, heaved her over the fence, where she fell

giggling in a heap on the lawn. I think they'd had enough of her and sent her back.

'I've been dwinking ouzo with Gwegowy Peck,' she announced, and then danced down the lawn towards the kitchen. Dad was furious as dinner was clearly off the menu. The fence is now known as the 'Pecking Fence'.

August 17th 1969

When I look at my life it's easy to compare myself to Superman. His real parents came from the planet Krypton and he was sent to Earth and adopted by a kindly Kansas farmer and his wife. He then discovered that he had special powers and that he was sent to Earth for a reason. To save the world from evil. If I'm being honest I think I'm very much like Superman. I've been sent here for a reason. I'm just not sure what my mission is...yet.

August 30th 1970

Went next door AGAIN because Uncle Gerry gave his spoilt daughter Tessa one of those new fangled Karryoki machines from Japan. We all had to sit on the floor while everyone took a turn to try and sing along to the words. It was all so ghastly I stood at the back with my arms folded. Then Tessa tried to sing a silly song called *Love Grows Where My Rosemary Goes* and I started to laugh. Uncle Gerry came and asked me why I was laughing.

'She was fabulous, but the singing was slightly offputing,' I said.

'Are you sure Simon?' he asked.

'Absolutely,' I said.

'Perhaps you would you like your turn now?'

'No thanks I can't sing.' After that Uncle Gerry
locked me out in the garden on my own. Sometimes
Uncle Gerry can be very rude...

August 31st 1970

I woke up and dad was shouting and swearing in the
garden. Mum said dad caught Bwana humping the
Corinthian columns and he's poohed all over the
rhododendron bush and now the whole garden has to
be redone. Mr Biggers wants to put wire fencing
round the bushes but Bwana keeps standing guard
outside the potting shed and won't let him out.

Dad says he might swap Bwana for a budgie.

September 13th 1971

— Are my parents planning to get rid of me?

Tonight I heard mum and dad kept having whispered discussions in the lounge about me. I couldn't quite make out what they were saying so I hid in the cupboard under the stairs to try and hear what they're talking about. Nanny Heather found me and told mum. Heather says I'm an odd boy and that it's not right for me to sit in cupboards when it's sunny outside.

Then mum found out that I'd been paying Nicholas to do my paper round, wash all the neighbours' cars and mow their lawns — jobs that she'd arranged for me to do. I thought she'd be impressed at my entrepreneurial flair. I told her that the key to great success is delegation and that I was managing my workload by making Nicholas do it and taking a large cut.

Now Nicholas says that mum and dad are so fed up

with me they're planning to send me away to a special school. Anyway I don't believe him. They wouldn't send *me* away, they love me best and I'm too bloody talented.

September 14th 1971

— My first smoke

Just to get me out of the house, mum made Tony take me to the cinema to see a film called *Dirty Harry* with Clint Eastwood. It was really great and Tony gave me my first cigarette. That was kind of him wasn't it? Now I can't stop smoking. Still, that's what brothers are for. Can't wait to find out what he's going to teach me next! Nothing good I'm sure.

September 25th 1971

Mum and dad have gone on holiday to a place called
Mauritius. Nanny Heather and Auntie Joan are
looking after us — which is much more fun and we
actually get fed properly.

I've just got a postcard from mum.

Dear Simon,

We are having a lovely holiday and I thought
you might want to know a little bit about the
place we are visiting.

Since independence in 1968, Mauritius has
developed from a low-income, agriculturally
based economy to a middle-income diversified
economy with growing industrial, financial
and tourist sectors. For most of the period,
annual growth has been of the order of five

OUR FIRST DRINK. NICHOLAS IS
WEARING HIGH SHOES TO LOOK
TALLER THAN ME.

to six per cent. And – get this – Mauritius was the only known habitat of the now extinct Dodo bird.

P.S. Today I went hang gliding and tomorrow I might go deep sea fishing.

Love Your mother xxx

October 10th 1972

SHOPPING LIST:

• CIGARETTES (B&H).

• SIX TINS OF TOP DECK SHANDY.

• A BLACK COMB.

• SOME BLACKHEAD REMOVER.

• THE NEW ROD STEWART SINGLE **YOU WEAR IT WELL.**

October 11th 1972

Mr Biggers told dad that he wants to redesign the garden. Ever since Bwana humped the Corinthian columns the whole structure has never been the same.

Dad and I found Mr Biggers sitting cross-legged in the potting shed fiddling with his tomato plants.

'So what do you suggest then Biggers?' asked dad.

'Well sir...I think the garden lacks a little passion, if you don't mind me saying so.'

'Well I don't want it turned into some sort of oriental theme park.'

'No sir. I was thinking more Greek than Far Eastern.'

'Very well. And I don't want the lawn changed either.'

'No sir. The lawn is like a poem sir...'

'Quite. How are the tomatoes coming along Biggers?

'Not too well sir — I think I've lost me magic touch sir.'

'Well don't give up Biggers — I'm looking forward to a bumper harvest.'

November 20th 1972

Dad took me to school this morning in the E. Type. As he shot out of the driveway I turned to him and said:'When I buy my sports car I'm going to get a black one.'

'Black's old fashioned son,' he said, firing up his first Cuban of the day.

'But dad, Uncle Gerry's Rolls Royce is black.'

'That's only because it's bloody old,' he barked, and turned up Perry Como.

February 7th 1973

Hooray! For the first time in my life I've just heard music coming from Tony's room that I actually *like*. He says it's a band called The Eagles — and I love it.

He let me sit in his room and listen to the whole record with him. But just to be on the safe side, while I was there I nicked all his favourite albums and hid them in the garage — behind the family bottle pile.

February 8th 1973

Can't believe that bloke Roger Moore has just got the part of James Bond! Are they serious? He can't even use a gun.

P.S. I just nicked one of dad's cigarettes from the lounge, they're called Sobranie. Yuk!

February 9th 1973

Uncle Gerry came round for dinner with another one of those American actors. A bloke called Robert Mitchum and he's got a huge great dent in his chin. He talks really slowly and mum laughs at everything he says. He asked me what I knew about America. I told him I thought there used to be lots of Red Indians over there before the cowboys shot them all. He then pulled a funny face and dashed to the toilet. I think I may have said something wrong.

February 10th 1973

Brother Tony has written this terrible book of poems and some deluded publisher has taken it on. I can't believe it. I'm no judge but the poems are all lovey-dovey — 'the sky is blue and so are you'. Appalling! I don't mean to be rude but they are just too funny. If

I'm being honest, Tony would be better off being an actor — like Sir Larry Grayson…

February 11th 1973

Mum has decided to have her bedroom re- designed — which I think is a good idea because at the moment it's all a ghastly purple colour and full of feathers. She's got one of those big books with all the different colours in. I told her she should do it all in white but I never realised how many shades of white you can actually get. I think one day I might paint my teeth a 'Brilliant Shiny white'.

12th February 1973

— The end of school as I knew it

Mum told me I'd got as bad at school as I was at home so I'd have to go away to boarding school because the teachers couldn't cope with me any more. They said I couldn't retain information, wouldn't do as I was told and had been incredibly rude to a science teacher. Some of this is true — particularly about the science teacher. I've simply come to the conclusion that learning about Newton's theory isn't exactly going to play a huge part in my future.

The thing about school is, I just don't see the point of it. I know how to read, I know how to write, and I know where America is. So what else do I need to know? I asked mum where the boarding school was and she said as far away as possible, which I didn't think was very funny. To be fair, it was always going to be hard to find any school willing to take me. But she found one: in Kent, called Stover High School.

She showed me the brochure and it looks like the house where Dracula lives. The slogan on the front of the brochure read: 'Helping develop individual talent.' Now what do I want to know about developing talent for? I might actually run away from home before I'm sent there. This is appalling behaviour from people who think they are good parents. I've just about had it with those two. And now I feel sick.

March 1st 1973

I've made my mind up to run away from home rather than go to that bloody school. Quite frankly, I'm done with school. There's nothing else I need to learn. I may as well get straight on with earning some money. This is all such a waste of time. I've warned my parents they're wasting their money. It would be better to spend it on buying me a car or a hotel. How can I earn money while I'm stuck in some crusty old school? There are no cars to clean — no wine bottles to clear up and no earnings from Auntie Joan. It's a disgrace. Some people should never have children if they don't listen to them.

March 14th 1973

— Leaving home

7.30 am. I've just done a deal with dad. He agreed that if I don't like Stover High I can come home again. (Yeah, like I really believe him.) And I no longer care what mum thinks — she's determined to get rid of me so she can carry on bug hunting and playing over the Pecking Fence with Liz Taylor. She really doesn't deserve to have a son like me. I'm so misunderstood.

I wedged my trunk into dad's E.Type and said goodbye to the dog and cat. I didn't feel like kissing mum goodbye so I just waved with two fingers from the car window. What does she care anyway?

I felt very sad as we drove away. I think dad felt the same way too, because as soon as we got down the drive he gave me a cigarette. As the smoke wafted round the car, I felt like a condemned man having his last cigarette before being shot.

8.30am — Dad dropped me off at King's Cross station and we said our goodbyes. He looked sad and even gave me ten cigarettes to take with me. I dragged my heavy trunk and made my way to platform nine. In the distance I could see the steam rising from the front of the train. A sign overhead said Stover High Express. The steam from the engine drifted overhead and a porter helped haul my trunk onto the train and slammed the door behind me.

I heard a whistle and the train began to chug slowly out of the station and I felt my stomach churn as I thought about my future. What bloody future do I have stuck in Stover High?

The first few carriages were packed with other kids on the train to hell. I found one empty compartment near the end of the train and kicked my trunk into it and slumped down on the seat. I smoked a cigarette and then began to drift off, dreaming idly about Bwana chasing Mr Biggers through a long dark tunnel, when suddenly the compartment door was flung open and there stood two huge boys with flaming red hair.

'SCOWELL!'

Christ, not the McDougal twins!

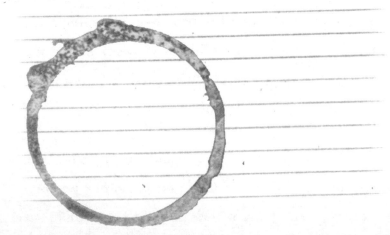

March 15th 1973

— Arriving at Stover High

What a bloody dump this is! It looks like a Victorian lunatic asylum. This is going to be hell. I already feel like a prisoner of war. A Miss Glowerbridge greeted us at the entrance to the school. She wore a long black cloak and her thin grey hair was pulled back behind her head. She glared at me.

'What's your name boy?'

'Cowell.'

'You mean Cowell, MISS.'

'Yes, Cowell Missssssssss.'

She ran a line through my name in a book and with a huge swish of her cloak turned and started to walk towards the huge dark towers of the school.

'Follow me Cowell.' she boomed.

As we climbed the stone spiral staircase I stared up at the scary paintings of what looked like dead headmasters. I followed Miss Glowerbridge as she shuffled down a long dark corridor and I struggled to keep up as I hauled my heavy trunk behind me. She stopped in front of an old oak door and pushed it with her shoulder and it opened with a loud creak. She stared down at me and grinned, pointing a bony figure towards an iron bed that lay beneath a small leaded window.

'Make yourself at home Cowell,' she hissed.

And with that she disappeared and the door closed behind her with a dull thud.

It was bloody freezing in the dormitory. How can parents be so cruel? They're going to regret sending me here. I felt so angry and resentful as I lay on my bed listening to the distant cry of the owl in the dark woods. So I decided to write to mum and dad and let them know how I felt:

Dear mum and dad

I hope you are happy to finally have got rid of me. I also hope you're comfortable in your warm, centrally heated house and you have a lot to eat. All I have is porridge and dry biscuits. And I am lying in a dormitory which has icicles on the inside. I'm freezing cold and hungry and I hope you are finally satisfied. You'd like it here mum because there are about 100 different cockroaches crawling all over my bed. Your behaviour has been totally unacceptable; you just don't deserve to be parents. Children are for life. You can't just send them away when it suits you. Oh, and give my love to Uncle bloody Gerry won't you?

From your former son — Simon

NOTE TO SELF:

MUST REMEMBER WHEN I AM REALLY RICH TO BUY MY PARENTS' HOUSE AND CHUCK THEM OUT ONTO THE STREET. HAH!

March 16th 1973

I had the most awful dream last night. Bwana became the hound of the Baskervilles and Miss Glowerbridge was a witch who married Mr Biggers and lived in the woods and made magic spells to turn boys into frogs.

At 7.59am Miss Glowerbridge unlocked our door and led us into the Grand Hall for assembly. The huge hall fell silent as the headmaster, Professor Fingerwood entered through a big door at the side of a stage followed by six masters dressed in black cloaks. He stood at the lectern and addressed the hall. He called out the names of the new boys and we all had to stand up.

He peered down at us and told us which houses we were going into.

I'm in Clifford House and guess what? So are the McDougal brothers...

March 19th 1973

5.31pm — Miss Glowerbridge came into my dorm and threw down a letter onto my bed and slammed the door behind her. It was from mum.

Dear Simon, Thank you for your lovely letter. I do hope you have now settled down at school and you are at last learning about things that may be useful to your future — and I don't mean Superman comics!

I hope you are using your encyclopedia I bought you. Look up the Spruce Bark Beetle because they have suddenly started to boom in Alaska thanks to 20 years of warm summers, and now the little blighters have chewed up 4 million acres of spruce trees?

The Mother

NOTE TO SELF:

ASK DAD TO STOP MUM'S SUBSCRIPTION TO
NATIONAL GEOGRAPHIC MAGAZINE.

March 26th 1973

— Stover High is a prison camp

They call Stover High a boarding school and now I
know why: I'm so bloody bored. The older boys beat up
the younger boys. The food is like wartime rations and
there are more rules than in the Highway Code. Miss
Glowerbridge comes round every morning and checks
our beds are made and the dormitory is clean (apart
from the cockroaches). The only good thing about this
place is there are about ten girls here. Not that any of
them would win a beauty contest but at least it's
something to look at. Though there is one girl called
Valerie Pincher who is quite cute.

I HAVE THREE GOALS:

- Smoke as many cigarettes as possible.

- Leave school at the earliest possible age.

- Avoid the McDougal brothers at all costs.

Things are going well with my second goal as me and five other boys have already been put in a special category because we're so useless. We've been given the option of either having special lessons with Miss Glowerbridge to improve our grades or learn to play tennis with Miss Viceroy. Suffice to say, my backhand is improving by the day.

NOTE TO SELF:

REMEMBER TO LOOK UP THE EARNINGS OF TOP TENNIS PLAYERS LIKE BJORN BORG.

March 27th 1973

A boy in my dorm called Ron Sleazeacre gave me a
book called *The Stud* by Jackie Collins.

'Have a shiftee at this Cowell,' he hissed. 'It's just
what the doctor ordered.'

All I can say is that it's much better than Jane
Austen and has loads of sex in it. So I'm going to send
it to brother Tony because I think he should write
books like this and he'll make loads more money than
writing silly poems.

March 28th 1973

Today we had our first French lesson. We learned how to say 'Hello, my name is...' The problem is that when I say my name in French it sounds like SIMONE — a bloody girl's name! Even Miss Glowerbridge found it funny. Everyone laughed and I was mortified. My parents clearly hate me. If I was a girl I expect they would have named me Paris or even Brooklyn. Yuk!

March 29th 1973

My class had to perform a play today in front of the whole school. And what a performance it was! I had to lie on the floor and play dead for the whole of the play. The only problem was for some reason I started to giggle so my 'dead' body was shaking throughout the show and everyone in the audience was laughing. Afterwards the drama teacher, Mr Lush, said that I was supposed to play dead — not *dead funny* and I had ruined the whole play and would never be allowed on stage again. Naturally I was absolutely delighted with the news and can't wait to tell mum. Even the McDougal twins came up to me and congratulated me on my performance.

April 2nd 1973

There's a kid in my dorm called Johnny Lopez. He's American and he's really interesting. He says that you can make much more money in America than you can here. Well, there's certainly no chance of making any money in Stover, that's for sure!

He says the dollar is more important that the pound — whatever that means. Anyway, Johnny says I should go and live in America because:

- There are more girls there

- The music's better

- The houses are much bigger

- You get paid more.

I think I might talk to Uncle Gerry about America once I get out of this bloody prison. I think America is where I could make my first million.

April 10th 1973

The good news is that cute girl Valerie Pincher has been put into our tennis group because she's crap at Physics. So I took her to one side this morning and told her I would be happy to show her my best drop shot. I feel I have a duty to pass on my expertise to her. Not that I needed to — this girl can really play. The girl's got talent.

April 15th 1973

— I get minders

I entered the Grand Hall at lunchtime and sat down next to Johnny Lopez. Immediately two large figures loomed into view and elbowed their way between Johnny and I and sat down at the table.

The room fell silent as I stared into two sets of red eyes that belonged to the McDougal brothers. It was no longer lunchtime — more like high noon. I reached out for the water jug and one huge hairy arm clasped my wrist tightly. His hot face moved closer to mine.

'Listen Scowell — me and my bruv have been thinking see. We loved your performance in the school play.'

'I'm so pleased you recognise talent when you see it,' I replied calmly.

'Aye... well, we think you're dead funny see, and if you

ever get into any trouble here at Stover we're gonna
be the ones who are going to look after you. Get it?'

'Well...yes. Thank you. I'll bear that in mind.'

A small murmur began to spread throughout the
great hall and the chattering returned. The
McDougals finished lunch, whacked me on the back
and marched out of the hall. I looked up at the tall
stained glass window at the end of the hall and said a
wee prayer to myself.

April 17th 1973

— 6.30pm

As I sat in my dorm and watched the cockroaches flitting to and fro I couldn't help but wonder what on earth will become of me? I hate school and I hate sitting in lessons pretending they are ever going to help me in my life.

Maths - why?

History — it's in the past

Physics — can you SEE velocity?

Science — I like Einstein's hair

Music — some is ok

Art — have done great picture of garden

Biology — what's pollen got to do with girls?

Chemistry — only fun when making test tube explode

All pointless. All a waste of time. It doesn't seem to add up. I need to find a way to escape from here...

April 20th 1973
— Reading aloud

Miss Glowerbridge said we all had to choose a book to read out loud to the whole class.

Johnny Lopez chose *Just William* about a boy who always gets into trouble at school. (So yesterday!) But some of the kids laughed at the bit where William puts salt into his mum's tea. Ron Sleazeacre wanted to read from a book called *Love in the Grass* but Miss Glowerbridge took it off him before he could start. Then she lowered her glasses and stared at me.

'And what are you going to read to us today Cowell?'

'Lord of the Flies Misssssssssssss.'

'My, what an interesting choice,' she said sarcastically.

'Well get on with it — we're all waiting.'

The room fell silent as I stood up slowly and pulled the book from my satchel and began to read.

When finally I'd finished reading everyone started to clap and Miss Glowerbridge almost smiled and said it was very good. Then she said: 'And what do you really like about Lord of the Flies Cowell?'

'Simple Miss,' I said. 'There are no bloody grown-ups in it.'

April 27th 1973

— In the Library

I'm beginning to like English and I needed inspiration
today so I went to find the library.

I made my way down the spiral staircase — avoiding eye
contact with the former heads from hell. This place was
like a rambling medieval castle from another world — a
giant warren of passages and dark corridors. It felt like I
had fallen through some strange time portal and I was
trapped in the castle of doom. At the foot of the huge
staircase I followed a sign to the library and found
myself in another dark winding corridor. At the end I
found myself standing in front of a huge oak door.

I pushed the door and slipped inside. I could hear the
sound of muttering and the flick of pages. I looked
around then moved softly in the direction of the sound.
Then I heard the low whisper:

'What do you want Cowell?' Ron Sleazeacre sat huddled in a corner with a huge book open on his lap. I stared at the title; *The Joy Of Sex* by Alex Comfort.

'Pity we're not allowed to take books back to the dorm,' he hissed, pointing to a sign on the wall.

'What are you after Cowell, something spicy?'

The Great Escape came to mind.

I smiled to myself and left Sleazeacre to his own devices and began my own search along the tall oak shelves. Then suddenly I saw it. I grabbed the book off the top shelf and sat down at one of the desks. I rubbed my finger slowly over the gold lettering of the title: *How To Be Really Honest* by JK Hartley. As I began to read I soon became totally absorbed in the book — and at that very moment all I could hear was the distant cry of the owl in the dark woods that lay beyond the school.

May 1st 1973

— Learning about the 'X factor'

Our music teacher, Mr Hammerdale said we should learn to appreciate different types of music and today he said he wanted us to talk about the songs we liked and bring in an LP.

I brought *Strangers in the Night* because it's got a lovely key change and you can tell when a song is good when it goes up in the middle. I also like the bit at the end when he sings 'doo be doo be dooooo'.

First, one of the McDougals played something noisy by the Bay City Rollers and we were asked to give our thoughts on it. I said: 'They should sue their singing teacher.'

'So what's your song then Scowell?' he hissed.

'Classy,' I said, walking over to the record player. 'And

a song that people will enjoy for hundreds of years to come.'

When Frank had finished Mr Hammerdale asked me to say what I thought.

'Well,' I said. 'I think the singer is unique and has star quality. It's that special something that you can't quite put your finger on...'

'I think it's called the "X factor" Cowell...' said Mr Hammerdale, whose eyes appeared to have misted over during my critique.

After the lesson Mr Hammerdale said he thought I had a real talent for music and a gift for saying what everyone in the room was thinking but was too scared to say.

If I'm being honest... I quite like music now.

MY MOST FAVOURITE SINGING PAIRS:

- DONNY AND MARIE OSMOND

- JERRY LEWIS AND DEAN MARTIN

- THE RIGHTEOUS BROTHERS

- FRANK SINATRA AND DORIS DAY

- SONY AND CHER

May 28th 1973

— Defining moments

Today I had another tennis session with Valerie
Pincher. We're now working on her backhand passing
shot. Back in the locker room she suddenly looked up
at me and asked me why I was helping her. I glanced
at my reflection in the mirror and smiled, sensing this
may be a defining moment:

'I guess I just recognise talent when I see it.' I said.

I saw her smile and flick her hair before she closed the locker room door behind her.

June 1st 1973

— A weird form of punishment

I'm in big trouble already! Last night I sneaked out of school and went into town for a beer with Johnny Lopez and the McDougal twins. Someone must have seen us and told the school because this morning we were hauled up in front of Professor Fingerwood. As the four of us stood shoulder to shoulder the headmaster paced the huge dark room as he read out, word for word, the meaning of rule 71 from the Stover High rulebook.

I held my breath because I feared the worst.

'You broke the rules,' he boomed.

'Tell me why I shouldn't cane you all Cowell?'

I thought for a moment. 'Well Sir, I believe in being honest,' I blurted out.

'And...if I'm being honest, I think the rules should at least allow us to go into town without a teacher say, once a week. It's all about freedom Sir...'

'**FREEDOM?**' he boomed.

The silence that followed was deafening. After what seemed like hours the headmaster slowly rose from his chair and picked up the cane that was lying on his desk and brought it down with a loud thwack on the back of his chair — and a fine dust filled the air.

Then he turned slowly to face the accused.

'Well, my boys... if it's freedom you really want you will all be suspended from Stover High for six weeks.

You may go!'

Outside in the hall Johnny Lopez jumped for joy and slapped me on the back.

'You saved us. You saved us,' he grinned.

The McDougal twins put their big red faces into mine and spoke in unison.

'You're a little wizard Scowell!'

Now I don't have to go back to school till after the summer hols. Whoopee! Can't wait to see mum's face when I get home.

June 2nd 1973

7.30am — As the train pulled into Stover station I
glanced back over the hill to see the sun rise over the
huge towers of the school. I kicked my trunk onto the
train and jumped in behind it. I just hoped that it was
dad and not mum that picked me up at King's Cross.
Mum will be furious but I know dad will understand.
As I looked out of the window as the train chuffed its
way through the boring fields of Kent I thought about
what Johnny Lopez had told me about America. I also
fingered the little note that Valerie Pincher had
slipped into my hand at the school gates.

I unfolded it slowly and began to read.

My dear Simon,

Just to let you know that Miss Viceroy says my drop volley has improved tremendously since you began to coach me and she says I should think about taking up tennis professionally when I leave school.

So, you see, I really have only you to thank. I think you have this wonderful ability to inspire people Simon, and you certainly know talent when you see it! You have a magic touch!

Be safe my little wizard.

Love Valerie.

June 6th 1973

— Hard labour back at Helstree

Not surprisingly I don't think mum is very pleased with me over this suspension. She appears to be giving me another form of punishment: it's called hard labour. She's made me chop down trees in the garden and clean the cars EVERY DAY! Dad seems pleased to see me though — and keeps giving me cigarettes to have in my rest breaks. Even Mr Biggers has started to share his egg sandwiches with me in the potting shed so things are looking up.

As I chopped down my 29th tree I couldn't help but wonder. One day I'm bound to be really rich and famous — and then I'm going to hire mum as my skivvy. Hah!

June 7th 1973

— I'm worried about Mr Biggers's toms

I found Mr Biggers in the potting shed this morning huddled over his tomatoes plants.

'What's the matter with your toms Mr Biggers? They don't look very healthy.'

'No Mr Simon, they never seem to grow — then they shrivel and die on the vine. I think I've lost my magic touch.'

He looked rather sad and stooped as he walked out into the orchard.

His tiny toms looked to me as if they suffered from the same plight as Nicholas. Short, stumpy and under nourished.

As I knelt down and gazed at the plants, I

accidentally tipped my Top Deck shandy all over the tomatoes and then tried to wipe them with my hands. Oh well, I thought, it can't be worse than Mr Biggers's miracle grow. So I tipped the rest of my shandy into his watering can.

June 8th 1973

I was allowed to watch television for the first time since I got home. So, will someone please tell me what *This Is Your Life* is all about? I've never seen anything quite so appalling on TV. Second-rate celebrities ranting on and on about how wonderful they are. It's sick-making. Can you just imagine being 'surprised' by that Eamonn Andrews? How embarrassing would that be?

June 15th 1973

Now that mum's calmed down a bit she took us out
to an Italian restaurant in Helstree called Sliprianis. I
like Italian food because it tastes nice. And Mr
Slipriani always brings me chips as well — which is
much better than all that roast pigeon stuff in prune
sauce that some people eat.

I think Italians know what they're doing with food. I
think mum should learn to cook like Mr Slipriani. She
certainly seems to spend more time there than in her
own kitchen!

After dinner mum announced that she's finally
decided to go to Africa to hunt for some silly rare
beetles. I looked at her in horror. 'Are you completely
mad woman?'

'It's just something I have to do dear,' she said.

Dad was furious and said he was only letting her go because she has agreed to take someone with her. So she's taking that posh lady from church — Dame Edith Shatwell who's got a big house where they're going to stay. I don't think she will be much help to mum — she so bloody fat she can't even bend down properly.

June 27th 1973

THINGS I MUST GET VERY SOON:

• PROPER AFRO COMB FOR MY HAIR.

• A CHOPPER BIKE.

• THE NEW DONNY OSMOND SINGLE *YOUNG LOVE.*

• MODEL EVEL KNIEVEL MOTORBIKE.

• BIGGER MIRROR

June 28th 1973

I've been playing with Bwana in the garden and
trying to get him to jump over chairs and tables like
they do in dog shows. Nicholas made a tunnel out of
an old carpet and Bwana had to run through it. I
think he'd be good on *That's Life* or a show for dogs
that have got a special gift.

July 5th 1973

          — I've pinned this up in the kitchen

PLEASE NOTE THESE ARE SIMON'S FAVOURITE DINNER:

- BIRDS EYE CHICKEN PIES
- FISH FINGERS AND CHIPS
- HEINZ SPAGHETTI HOOPS
- HEINZ BEANS ON TOAST
- CHIPS (NOT YOURS MUM, FROZEN ONES!)

August 9th 1973

Mum finally left for Africa today with Dame Edith Shatwell. They are going to look for Aardvarks whatever *they* are. Then they're off to Madagascar to hunt for cockroaches. Dad says we have to let her do what she wants but I think she's bloody barmy. She'll only come back with the lurgy. But I can't say I'm sorry to see her go at least now we might get some proper food to eat. After lots of tears (mum's not mine), Dad drove her to the airport and before she left Mr Biggers gave her a whole new set of jars to put her bugs in.

Women!

August 12th 1973

Over dinner (which for once was edible) Dad told me Nicholas wants to go into the property business like him. Great I said, it will suit him down to the ground. It's boring, dull and full of people with no sense of style. I plan to do something much more exciting and make a million well before Nicholas does.

Dad says I'm just greedy and I should stop dreaming and start thinking about a proper career. Then he said that now this Edward Heath bloke is Prime Minister things can only get better in Britain.

'Well,' I said, 'they can't get any bloody worse can they?'

August 20th 1973

Didn't sleep that well at all last night. Brother Tony's back for the weekend and being his usual annoying self. Most of the night all I could hear was the sound of Pink Floyd tinkering their way through *Dark Side of the Moon*. Does he ever go to bloody bed?

September 3rd 1973

Dad let me stay up late because he knew I had to go back to Stover High in the morning.

Uncle Gerry came round to see dad tonight. I think he wants to look after him because mum's away. He brought another one of those actors with him called Trevor Howard. He spoke very posh and gave me two quid. Dad said he was very famous because he was in a film called **Brief Encounter**. Then Dad put a Jack Jones LP on and they all ate loads of cheese and drank port, and filled the lounge with a huge fog from their cigars.

Tonight I feel like running away forever.

September 4th 1973
— Back to Stover High

This morning, as the sun rose, I loaded my trunk into Dad's E. Type and he drove me to King's Cross station. He was very quiet during the journey but I think that was something to do with the port and cheese.

At the station he gave me £2 and ten cigarettes and told me to try and keep out of trouble.

As I made my way to platform nine the thought of going back to school depressed me. I can't wait for these exams and then I'll be free of the bloody place for ever. I'm going to make sure I screw up every exam except English – just in case dad has plans for me to become a scientist or an estate agent. Now he says I could always get a part-time job working as a waiter when I finish school but we'll see about that. If I'm being honest, I have a funny feeling that waiting tables isn't the career for me. But what is I wonder...?

September 5th 1973

When I arrived back at Stover High, Johnny Lopez was waiting for me at the gate. He looked all hot and bothered. He blurted out that there was this new girl at school called Concheeta and she's really cute and one of the McDougal brothers was already trying to date her.

'What's that got to do
with me?' I asked.

'Everyone's calling you the wizard.'

'Jesus'...

By the time I'd hauled my trunk back to my dorm
both McDougals were waiting for me. 'What do you
know about music Scowell?' asked the love struck
one.

'Absolutely nothing I'm afraid.' They both looked at
each then back at me.

'The school concert is next month and Concheeta is
a good wee singer but she hasn't got a song to sing. I
need to find her one then she'll really like me. I'm
shit at music so I need to find someone who can help
me, and you're top of my list.'

'But I can't **write** songs I'm crap at music too.' I pleaded.

'Well friggin find someone who can.' He boomed, getting up from the bed.

'We want this girl to have the best chance of winning. Right?'

'Right.'

The door slammed behind them.

I still don't understand girls.

September 6th 1973

— Miss Glowerbridge arrived with
the mail this morning.

It was another letter from Mum:

Dear Simon

We landed in Cape Town yesterday and we're off to Dame Edith Shatwell's house to inspect her melons. On Monday we go into the African bush to search for Aardvarks. A camera crew have just arrived dear, and they want to film me doing it! Is'nt that great? I've always wanted to be on television.

Please look after Nicholas and tell Nanny Heather to make sure he eats — I'm still very worried about his lack of height.

P.S. Did you know that an Aardvark's tongue can grow up to 12 inches long?

Love

The mother

September 10th 1973

I think my luck's in — I've found this really nerdy kid
called Pete Blackman who's in the year below me —
he always comes top in music and wins all the school
prizes; *and* he writes his own songs! So I grabbed him
after assembly to try and persuade him to write a
song for this Concheeta.

'The thing is mate I just do pop,' he said, squinting
through tiny wire framed glasses.

'Fine, well do you think you could write a sort of pop
ballady thing. It's for a girl.'

'I could try mate.'

'Thanks Pete. But we're going to need it in time for
the school concert.'

'No problem mate. Hey, what's in it for me?'

'Fame?'

Later, back in my dorm, I couldn't help but wonder;
it's all very well choosing the right song but I hope
this girl can actually sing...

September 12th 1973

Miss Glowerbridge took me to one side this morning
and said that I appear to have no talent for learning.
So I told her I really couldn't understand the point of
school.

'At what point in my life would I ever need to know
the outcome of mixing sodium hydroxide with
phosphorous acid?' I asked her. She glared at me and
stormed off down the corridor. And, if I'm being
honest, she didn't really have an answer did she?

September 14th 1973

In our music lesson today Mr Hammerdale told us all about song structures. Verses, choruses, middle eights and bridges. It was all very interesting but I felt like somehow I already knew all this. So I put my hand up.

'Yes Cowell?'

'I think the hook is the most important aspect of a song sir.'

'Really? And what is the hook Cowell?'

'It's that magic part of a song that makes you remember it sir. All the best songs have it.'

'You mean like *Chirpy Chirpy Cheep Cheep*?'

'If I'm being honest, I was thinking more *Without You* sir.'

ONE OF MUM'S FUNNY HATS

'Good... good. Well done Cowell. I'm sure that one day everyone will come to admire your musical tastes.'

September 25th 1973

As I consider my future, the one thing I know for sure is that I'm not going to look to my schoolmates for an example. Most kids at Stover High want to take a year off to travel the world. That's not an option for me. I have no desire to hike across the dusty plains of Australia without a hairdryer.

I want to earn money, not waste my time. My dad is already panicking about my future. I've just had a letter from him asking if I would consider training as a builder when I leave school. I've just written back to him because he's clearly not very well:

Dear dad

Are you mad?

Love Simon.

School has taught me one thing. Academic qualifications count for nothing. I've been thinking lately about whether a career in the entertainment business might suit me. Uncle Gerry, for all his bad habits, has given me a taste for the high life. If I'm being honest I'll leave this place with nothing but an overdeveloped ego — so I might be qualified for this type of work. I'm going to write to Uncle Gerry tonight — as soon as I've finished my tennis lesson with Valerie Pincher.

October 1st 1973

This kid Pete Blackman has finally finished writing the song for Concheeta. It's called *Not a Moment Too Soon* and it's fantastic! It sounds like opera and is really romantic. So I rushed it over to McDougal's dorm after school and showed it to him. He sat on his bed and sang it very quietly to himself with his big red head turned to the wall. Then, when he had finished, he looked up at me and frowned.

'It's a bit of a wee corny ballad — are you sure this will work?'

'Trust me — it will work. Girls love ballads.'

'Aye...well you'd better be right Scowell!'

I stood up to leave and then turned back to face him, one hand on the door.

'Can I give you one more piece of advice?' I asked.

'What is it?'

'Make sure Concheeta is the last one to perform at the concert.'

McDougal stared blankly at me and then stuffed the song into his pocket.

'By the way,' I added. 'Can she actually sing?'

'That dinna matter nowadays Scowell. You should know that.'

October 6th 1973

I played tennis with Valerie Pincher this morning; we're working on her backhand passing shot. Boy, this girl is one hell of a fast learner. I think I've got a potential

Wimbledon champion on my hands. In the locker-room afterwards she turned to me and said:

'Simon. Can I ask you something?'

'Sure. What is it?'

'Will you be going to the Halloween dance after the concert?'.

'Maybe, if I'm not working.'

'The thing is; I wondered whether you would come as my partner.'

'Yes, yes...we'll see.'

A shaft of sunlight caught the side of her face and she looked up at me and smiled. She reminded me of Bwana, when he was a puppy.

Later that night in my dorm I couldn't help but

wonder. I like Valerie but I don't want to rush into anything because girls can be trouble. They distract you. And I need to leave here as soon as possible and make some money fast. All that girl stuff...well... that will have to wait. My career comes first, once I've thought of one.

October 7th 1973

It was my birthday today but I didn't want to make a fuss so I never told anyone at school. I did get a card from dad, Nicholas and brother Tony but that was about it. Besides I'm so busy here trying to pull this whole concert together. I suddenly feel as if I have a mission — a purpose in life.

Though I've yet to fathom how I'm ever going to make any money from it.

October 12th 1973

— 5pm my dorm

After lessons the McDougals burst into my dorm.

'We need your help Scowell...'

'Not again. I'm washing my hair.'

'We need you to listen to Concheeta.'

'I *told* you — I'm not a good judge of singers — ask Pete Blackman — he's the expert.'

They both moved closer and I could feel the heat from their faces.

'Listen Scowell... we think it's *you* that has the magic touch.'

'Is that so? Well, I won't be bullied into this — and besides, it's you that has a vested interest in her — if she wins what do I get out of it?'

They looked at each other before speaking:

'Ok...' says love struck, 'if she wins we'll pay you. If she doesn't we won't.'

'That's more like it. Where is she?'

'In the music room, follow us...'

6.30PM

The much loved diva was perched on a stool by the window with a small hairbrush in her hand. The McDougals gathered round her protectively. My god, I thought, I can see what all the fuss is about. This girl was stunning.

'So what's the problem?' I asked, looking into her huge dark eyes. She looked me up and down before speaking: 'I think the song's too high for my voice.'

'I see...' I said, trying to avoid her gaze.

'Can you sing it for me please?'

When she started singing I felt my whole body lift off
the ground and I think all my hair stood on end. She
had the voice of an angel and a face to match.
When she had finished the room was silent. The
McDougals stared at me with their arms folded. I
coughed. 'It's in the wrong key — that's all. Try
singing it in D.' She did — and it was note perfect. At
the end she looked at me and smiled. My feet felt
like lead weights and were stuck to the floor.

'You reckon she could win?' Asked the love struck
McDougal.

'Well,' I said. 'She stands a very good chance indeed.'

The earth had moved.

October 17th 1973

Miss Glowerbridge delivered my mail this morning —
and for the first time she smiled at me, and showed
her yellow teeth. What on earth is going on here…?
There must be something in the water. Anyway here's
the letter:

My Dear Simon,

I'm bored with looking for Aardvarks and I'm
now in Madagascar because I wanted to go
and see if I could find that hissing cockroach
— or Gromphadorhina Portentosa to give it its
real name — if you want to look it up. But
you'll never guess what? I think I've
discovered a completely new breed of
cockroach and I'm so excited.

I caught one of the little blighters in Dame Edith Shatwell's slippers so I've put it in a matchbox and sent it off to be authenticated. It doesn't hiss dear but makes a clucking sound with its teeth so, if I'm right, I may have found a hitherto unknown species. I'm going to call it the Madagascan clucking cockroach.

By the way- happy birthday darling I've enclosed a postal order for you. I'm so sorry if it's late but the post is awful here.

All my love

The mother

October 18th 1973

I was lying on my bed thinking about Concheeta when
Johnny Lopez tapped me on the shoulder. He was
holding a book.

'Hey Cowell, you know what? America has a much
deeper pool of cultural talent than Britain. We've got
Elvis, Sinatra, Hemingway, Bo Diddly, Brando, Marvin
Gaye, Scorsese, Steinbeck, Stevie Wonder, Dean Martin,
The Jackson Five, John Wayne, Johnny Cash, Dionne
Warwick, Rock Hudson, Barbara Streisand and Clint
Eastwood.'

'Yea, that's true,' I said.

'But you also have Richard Nixon.'

October 31st 1973

— The night of the school concert

6PM — My dorm is like a mad house. Everyone was dashing in and out. First there was Johnny Lopez, who right at the last moment decided he wanted to sing *Unchained Melody* but didn't know the lyrics — so I had to write the words on his shirt cuffs. Then the McDougals arrived and asked me what I thought Concheeta should wear. Then, right in the middle of everything, Miss Glowerbridge burst in.

'Who do you think's going to win tonight Cowell?' she asked.

'I've no idea,' I said. 'I'm a lousy judge.'

7.30PM — The Grand Hall looked magnificent. There were Jack-o-lanterns everywhere and all the teachers were dressed as ghouls and zombies — just another day at the office then! Johnny Lopez went on first and predictably he was crap and got booed off the stage. Next came Miss Viceroy who sang *The Sound of Music* which all sounded a bit prim — though Professor Fingerwood applauded a little too long. Then four girls who called themselves the Vice Girls sang *That'll Be The Day* and suddenly the whole place went absolutely wild.

I ran backstage to find the McDougals in the girls' toilets shouting at Concheeta to get dressed. She looked ashen. I glared at the twins. 'Stop bullying her!' I boomed, and they quickly parted to let me through.

I sat Concheeta down and told her I thought the show was hers for the taking — and that she could easily win. She looked down at her feet and said, 'But I think everyone likes the Vice Girls.' I lifted her face up. 'Concheeta, just listen to me. When you sing, look directly into the eyes of the audience.'

'Will that help Simon?' she asked.

'Yes, like magic. Now pull yourself together and get out there.'

As the first bars of *Not a Moment Too Soon* began the audience were still muttering. Professor Fingerwood made a loud Schusssssssssssh and the room fell silent. Out walked Concheeta and stood in the single spotlight on the stage. As she opened her mouth to sing I looked across the Grand Hall and saw both McDougals with their arms round each other transfixed. I smiled to myself and as Concheeta reached the final key change the whole school was on its feet. When she finished there was no doubt in my mind who had won. This girl could be a star.

The moment Professor Fingerwood announced Concheeta the winner she came running over to me and flung her arms round my neck.

'Simon — I just wanted to thank you. Without you I would never have won. You really are a wizard.'

The earth moved again.

9PM. OUTSIDE THE GRAND HALL.

I was having a sneaky smoke and watching the bats swerve and swoop low over the lake. The moon was full and the sky was studded with stars. Suddenly I felt a tap on my shoulder and I swung round. There stood Valerie Pincher looking like a young Doris Day. Her hair pulled back in a pony tail. She looked up at me and smiled:

'Shall we go to the dance?'

I stubbed out my fag and she tried to put her arm through mine but I pushed it away and walked in ahead of her.

Back in the Grand Hall the McDougals had sneaked some beer in which they decantered into Coke bottles. Then we all cringed as Miss Glowerbridge and Professor Fingerwood tried to dance to Suzy Quattro.

The weird thing was, I reckon this Pete Blackman can't stop writing songs. As the dancing began he came over and pinned me to the wall and shouted in my ear.

'If you ever want a song for your girl I've got just the one mate?'

'Really?' I said. 'What's it called?'

'Come on over to Stover Val..er..ie...'

November 12th 1973

I was lying in my dorm thinking about Concheeta and
what Johnny Lopez had said about America. It's true
they do have an enormous pool of talent. But they
also have more bloody people. Maybe I should
consider working there — but doing what? Ever since
the Beatles went there they really love the British.
Maybe I could be a fashion designer or make films
like Alfred Hitchcock. Maybe I could be a talent
spotter — find the next Elvis Presley or Frank Sinatra.
When I was a kid I remember asking Uncle Gerry just
how much money they make from selling all those
records. And it's a lot!

Anyway, one day I'm going to be king of the world.
That's for sure!

I was so happy the concert went well and Concheeta
won fairly. If I'm being honest, without me it would

have been a complete shambles. So, last night I wrote to Dad and told him I have made a decision to leave school. However, I'm not expecting an immediate response.

December 1st 1973

— So today I got a letter from mum instead...

My Dear Simon, Just to let you know I'm home now with your father. And guess what? I was right after all. I have found a new species of cockroach. Your mother has officially discovered the Madagascan clucking cockroach. So now I'm going to phone that Attenborough chap. Not the one in films, the other one, and see if he wants to come and look at it. By the way, that nice man from the TV company said they might put me on television. I could be the next David Bellamy but without the silly voice.

Dame Edith Shatwell said I should call the show Bug Idol but I think that's really silly don't you?

I'm looking forward to seeing you at christmas and I'm going to cook you all a lovely meal while dad talks to you about your future...!

All my love

The mother

I can't bloody wait...!

December 12th 1973

It all felt a little strange breaking-up for Christmas. If I'm being honest I didn't think I would be back here next term. But I still had mixed feelings. I'd miss my chums at Stover but not the boring lessons. I came bottom in all my exams apart from English. I excelled at tennis and now appear to have a huge following amongst the pupils. Professor Fingerwood even asked me to give a speech on the last day of term to the 1st Year's. I called it *The Importance of Being Honest*.

After my speech, I went outside the Grand Hall to have a smoke. The moon was high in the sky and the lake was shrouded in mist as Professor Fingerwood suddenly appeared from nowhere. I stubbed my fag out on my shoe and he asked me if I'd ever thought about going into politics when I left school. I told him I didn't think there was much call for honesty in politics. Besides, I

said, I'm thinking of doing something in the entertainment business…just don't ask me what.

He appeared confused and his rheumy eyes looked sad and tired. Then, rather awkwardly, he put one arm around my shoulder and whispered in my ear.

'Whatever you choose to do boy, I know you will do it well. Oh, and by the way, we've decided to change that rule book after all.

God bless you Cowell.'

And with that he turned his back and disappeared into the mist.

I HATE WEDDINGS!
BUT CHECK OUT MY EXTRA
LONG FRINGE.

December 14th 1973

— My dorm
— for the last time?

I was in my dorm packing my trunk when Valerie burst in the door. Her face looked pinched.

'Are you catching the early train?' she gushed.

'I'm getting the *only* train.'

Her face became even more pinched.

'Can I come with you?'

A scene from *Brief Encounter* came to mind. 'I thought you were staying till the 16th?' I said.

'I was but...I thought I'd come with you.'

I looked up into her long face.

'Look Val, I'm not... you know... I don't have any

romantic plans at the moment. I need to find my own way.'

'But you *will* Simon. I ~~know~~ you will. You possess an extraordinary power and you must follow your chosen path to success. I just wanted to say thank you for all you've done to help me.'

Our eyes met for what I thought may be the last time.

She walked slowly towards the door, her head down — then stopped and turned her sad face towards me:

'I will never forget you Simon....good luck.'

I couldn't look.

As the door closed behind her I heard the school bell in the distance. In the chapel the First Year choir began singing *Little Town of Bethlehem* and I looked out through the small leaded window and watched the snow fall silently on the lake.

February 4th 1974

- Back to reality
- Helstree

When dad picked me up from King's Cross he didn't look very happy.

'What's the matter with you?' I asked, as I heaved my trunk into the back seat of the E. Type.

'I've just had the head of the Animal Planet TV on the phone. They've offered your mum a million quid to have her own TV series.'

'Are you serious? Rather, are they serious?'

'Both I'm afraid. That Attenborough chap has sold them on this whole bug thing. They want her to present her own show and now she's going to be a big star.'

'No way! Well I suppose it's better then going on *Come Dancing*.'

'But it's all gone to her bloody head,' he moaned, and pulled out into the Euston Road.

'She even wants to get her own PR man.'

'Oh well,' I said, 'I suppose she's got to sell herself to the max.'

As we hit the A40 Dad fired up a Cuban and floored the accelerator on the E. Type.

'The thing is,' he said, 'I'm just not sure I can cope with her ego once she goes on television.

Oh, and by the way, your brother Nicholas wants to shack up with a girl called Dorothy.'

Christ, I wished I'd stayed at school...

February 12th 1974

— Girls and all that stuff...

I've discovered that girls find me very attractive. I don't know what to do about it. I was at the pub last night when a hot-looking blonde girl approached me. 'Hello, I'm Cindy,' she gushed. Most of my ginger beer spurted down my nose and I went completely puce. Cool start I thought.

The next thing I know she is sitting on the back of my new moped as we sped down the country lanes back to her house. The moment we got in the door she starts to rip my clothes off. The problem was I still had my crash helmet on and I ended up naked with my T-shirt stuck over my helmet.

'Let's have a bath together,' she said. Good idea I thought, I'd got mud-splattered riding my moped... After a few minutes she jumped out of the bath and ran out shouting: 'Come into the bedroom in five minutes'. Strange girl I thought, she hasn't even dried her hair properly. This made me think she didn't really care too much about her image. Which of course I do. Image is so important if you want to get on in life.

Suddenly I felt quite agitated. I wasn't sure what I was supposed to do next. There was nobody to turn to — nowhere to run. Oh well, I thought, here goes...I dried my hair, got dressed and knocked gently on her bedroom door. Twenty minutes later I was back on my moped heading back to the pub. Blimey — bath nights were never like this! I was a bit shaky on the moped going home that night but I had a feeling that, with a bit more practice, I could get definitely get used to this girl thing.

I think it's a bit like riding a bike actually...

NOTE TO SELF: MUST TELL NICHOLAS. HE'LL BE SOOO JEALOUS.

March 15th 1974

— Mum comes over all TV...

The next morning dad called me into the study and I sensed trouble.

He told me he had caught mum in her dressing room talking into a mirror and holding a hairbrush like a microphone. He said she looked odd and was speaking with a plummy voice like a newsreader. 'It's all going to be a bloody nightmare,' he said in a sort of stage whisper.

He fired up a Cuban, poured himself a large gin and walked slowly towards the window.

'I blame that Desmond Morris bloke. Women belong in the kitchen and not on television. I don't understand why anyone would want to go on television and make a fool of themselves. This family will be a laughing stock. We're Cowells not bloody Attenboroughs. God knows

what they'll think of me at the Conservative Club.
Perhaps you should talk to her — see if you can change
her mind?'

While his back was turned I swiped a B&H from the
silver case on his desk.

'I'll try dad,' I said, 'but she's convinced she's got talent.'

'So what?' he growled. The whole of bloody Britain
think they've got talent.'

March 16th 1974
‑‑‑‑‑‑‑‑‑‑‑‑‑‑‑‑‑‑
— Success at last for Mr Biggers

As I opened the door of the potting shed Mr Biggers
shot up from beneath the tomato vine.

'Look at the size of this Mr Simon....you'll never
believe it.' He held up the biggest, reddest tomato I had
ever seen. It was the size of an orange, only red.

'I just don't understand it. One minute they're all small and wrinkled and now.....well.'

'Did you change the feed Mr Biggers?'

'No...been using the same old stuff from me watering can and giving them a good rub from time to time.'

I stared up at the giant plant that now filled the potting shed. Every single tomato was the same size. Absolutely massive!

'It's a miracle young Simon. Nothing short of a miracle.'

'I've had the man from the Horticultural Society ere this morning. He wants me to show them straight away at the Chelsea Vegetable Show —says I might win a prize.'

'But Mr Biggers — you've got talent. I'm no judge but I reckon you'll win hands down.'

He smiled and turned back to his giant toms muttering to himself. 'Nothing short of a miracle...'

As I left him rubbing his toms I couldn't help but wonder: There are definitely other things out there which can make you happy. And then of course there's money!

March 17th 1974

— I give mum a critique

Mum was due to start filming today and she was running all over the house in a massive flap.

She bursts into my room.

'Where's my hair curlers Simon? My car arrives in twenty minutes.'

'I've no idea. Try Nicholas's bedroom.'

'Look' she says. Can you get up please I need your advice on what to wear?'

I threw on a dressing gown and followed Mrs Panic into her dressing room.

'What do you think about this?' she says, holding up a khaki trouser suit with a huge belt attached.

'You look like one of the creatures that live in the jungle with the massive eyes,' I said. 'Why don't you go for something a bit more feminine?'

'Because I'll be crawling around in rocks looking for bugs. And I can hardly do that wearing six inch stilettos.'

'Actually, mum I think you're wrong. You've got to think of your audience — what the viewers want to see. Times are changing and people really love to see fashion. Just think of the ratings.'

'Do you really think so dear? Then what about this Dior trouser suit that Liz Taylor bought me?'

'Perfect.'

March 18th 1974

— It's different for girls

I've been thinking more about girls than about my future. The biggest problem with girls is they talk — I hate it that they simply don't agree with what I say. Why not? I'm always right. I wish they were more like dogs — obedient, loyal, loving but don't talk. I'm not sure about all that licking though. Come to think about it, cats and terrapins don't say much either. I think it might be easier if I wrote a list of rules for them before starting on any sort of long-term relationship. Not that I'm thinking of starting any long-term relationship — though, if I'm being honest..

VALERIE V CONCHEETA — JUST WEIGHING UP THE DIFFERENCES

VALERIE

- Fit — as in sporty

- Likes to talk about 'us' — yeuch — why?

- Disagrees with me a lot

- Does those puppy eyes thing which is very nice

CONCHEETA

- Fit — not as in sporty

- Happy go lucky

- Disagrees with me sometimes

- Wears some very unusual clothes

Anyway what's the point of all this. Making money is

definitely more important than girls. I'm going to rip these pages out of my diary because I don't want them found.

August 21st 1974
— Dad's little boring chats...

It's one of those days again. Dad's been thinking about my future. I'm sure he means well but hey, this is my life and I'm going to do exactly what I want with it.

I was sitting in my bedroom listening to the new Fleetwood Mac album when dad bursts in and signals with his pipe to turn down the music. He sits down on my yellow bean bag and almost topples backwards, which was a cool start. I knew there was a sermon on the way and it was bound to have the same effect on me as listening to one of his Perry Como records — bloody boring.

August 22nd 1974

— Dad's idea of a perfect job
— Number one.

Dad came up with a cunning plan to kick-start my career and lined me up with a host of job interviews he organised through his mates. This is going to be torture because he has this weird notion that I'd benefit by following in his muddy footsteps into the building trade. 'It's better than doing nothing son,' he said. Wrong, I thought.

To keep the peace, I agreed to attend a TWO DAY training course to study building materials. (I can't believe I've just said that!) So there's a teacher, pointing to an overhead projector image of some concrete. 'What are the properties of concrete?' he asks.

'I think it's not a good look and I don't think it's got what it takes.'

'But it's very functional,' said the instructor.

'I think it's grey, it's dull and it's not a winner'

'This isn't a talent competition, Mr Cowell!'

As we drove home from Swindon dad said, 'I take it you're not interested then?'

'NO, NO, NO. NO. NO!'

'Well, just give me a reason why not?' he pleads.

'I have six thousands reasons, dad,' I tell him. 'Can we please go home NOW so I can wash my hair?' He lit a Cuban and fired up the E-type. We spent the next few hours in complete silence apart from the constant roar of the V12. I knew he was really annoyed as he didn't even stop at the Happy Eater on the way home.

August 30th 1974
— Mr Biggers wins a prize

Mr Biggers took his toms to London this morning. Nanny Heather helped him load them all into his van and then decided to go up with him. They phoned dad at 4pm and sounded very excited.

'Well did you win Biggers?' asked dad.

'I did indeed sir. I won the top prize. And they had the BBC there and I'm on the news tonight sir.'

'Good show Biggers. I always knew you had it in you.'

They didn't get home till very late last night. I heard Mr Biggers's van chug up the driveway and I ran downstairs and peered through the kitchen window. They seemed to be sat in the van for what seemed like ages then, finally, Nanny Heather came in and ran straight upstairs giggling. Her face, I noticed, was as red as Mr Biggers's toms!

September 22nd 1974

— Dad's idea of the perfect job
— Number Two

Dad's next brilliant idea was to get me an interview with a supermarket. (Yawn).

He told me that he could get me on to a trainee course, where the pay was quite good. He said I would soon go on to become a regional store manager.

Mum of course wanted me to go to 'keep the peace' so off I bloody go again. I arrived at Supermarket HQ and was quickly ushered into the world's smallest office. Behind the desk sat the world's most boring man. What a combo! His hair was combed over his head to hide his bald patch, and before I could sit down he was already looking me up and down like a pervert.

'Why are you wearing jeans?' was his first and last question.

'Because I always wear jeans,' I replied. 'Don't you like them?'

The silence was deafening. At last he said, 'I actually don't think you have management potential.' A very acute observation.

'Really?' I asked, with my head on one side. 'Are you sure you don't want to reconsider?'

'No, definitely not,' he replied.

'Marvellous. I'm off then.' As I got up to walk out, I turned to him and said,

'As a matter of fact you need to know that I had no intention of ending up as a middle-aged bore, sitting in an office the size of a toilet. And I slammed the door behind me. So much for supermarkets — bring back the corner shop I say. The cheek of the man.

October 7th 1974

— Another bloody birthday

I suddenly feel very old. I wasn't even bothered what
birthday presents I had got.

Think I'm depressed. Spent most of the morning laying in
bed weighing up my options.

- Go back to school? — don't think so

- Wait on tables? — would have to be nice to people

- Become an Estate Agent? — get stuffed!

- Be a tennis coach? — not enough money

- Go to drama school? — yuk!

- Become a pop star? — can't sing

- Work in films? — possible...

- Go into politics? — too bloody dull

- Be an entrepreneur like Richard Branson. Possibly, but I don't like beards or funny jumpers

- What about working in television? — definitely not

January 12th 1975
— Opportunities at the post office...

Believe it or not, he thinks it would be a great idea for me to apply for a job in the Post Office. We are now deeply entrenched in the world of the 'Carry On' films. Quite frankly, it was the most bizarre idea I'd ever heard of in my short life. Even mum couldn't help but stifle a giggle when I told her. I said to her, 'Do I look as if I'm cut out to be a postman?'

'You're not cut out for anything dear.'

'So why the hell am I being sent for an interview?'

'Your father's only trying to help dear'

'No he's not — he's trying to ruin my life!'

On the day of the interview, a woman (who looked a bit like Miss Glowerbridge) handed me a fact sheet which showed the huge earning potential within the Post Office. By the time I'm 65 I could be earning £12,000 a year. Can you buy an Aston Martin for that? I don't think so.

So, I was told to sit outside in this drafty hallway and fill out a form the size of a telephone directory. That morning I had made the mistake of borrowing one of Tony's ties. As I looked down, I noticed to my horror it had a dagger motif all over it. I looked like a serial killer! Ha ha. After hours of waiting, I was summoned into a huge dark room, to be faced with a panel of three stony-faced judges.

'What is it that you find attractive about the post office?' asked the first judge.

'Well, I'm no judge but although I think it's better than last year, I don't know if it will realise its dreams and I'm interested in international success and that's what I'm looking for,' I replied.

'Sorry?' he asked, looking like he'd just eaten a pickled egg.

'I think you have to judge everything based on your personal taste. And if that means being critical, so be it.'

The interview was short and luckily, I didn't get the job. (Don't know why I kept saying judge there — I meant, interviewer.)

June 4th 1975

At last, dad finally conceded defeat in his bid to take my career to new lows. At the same time he confided in mum that he had a sneaking suspicion I had sabotaged every job interview he had sent me to. No way!!

Auntie Joan came round and said she would give me a fiver if I cleaned up the empty wine bottles out of the garage. It sounded like a good deal until I looked at the pile and realised I might need a bulldozer. Still, I'm going to need the money now...

Later in the evening I decided to announce to dad that I **might** try and get into the film business. I'm sure Uncle Gerry would help me. To avoid any discussion I decided to get straight to the point. I stuck my head round the door of his study and yelled:

'I think I might go into the film business. And guess what? You don't need a physics O level to do it.' I just had time to see his gin glass slip through his fingers before I slammed the door.

NOTE TO SELF:

IF YOU WANT TO GET ON IN LIFE — DON'T RELY ON ANYONE ELSE TO HELP YOU.

September 15th 1976
— Moving out of Helstree?

What's also really annoying me is that Nicholas has just left college and got a job with dad as an estate agent and he's earning £250 a week with a company car! And now he wants to move into his own flat with this Dorothy Lovechop or whatever her name is — and now he's bought a puppy and called it Prancer.

He's just so smug I'm going to have to find a way to wipe that smile off his face. Now I think maybe I should leave home. But then again I think it's too soon. Besides who the hell would I get to cook for me?

I wonder where that Valerie Pincher is?

December 3rd 1976

Mum made me work part-time as a waiter in this crap restaurant just to please dad. I'm lousy at waiting on tables, the tips are awful and it's so hard being nice to people. The end came quite suddenly and hilariously when this guy ordered liver and bacon. I was putting the plate down on his table and the liver, together with the onion gravy, slithered on to his lap. The fact that he was wearing cream-coloured trousers didn't help matters either. What an appalling taste in fashion — it was probably an improvement! I've had enough of all this table waiting. I've got to get a proper job.

This morning at breakfast I told mum that if I didn't go into the film business than maybe I might try the music business; and she promptly dropped the butter dish all over the floor.

'And what do you know about the music business?' she asked.

'I'm bloody sure I can find better bands than Brotherhood of Man,' I told her.

And this new punk music is appalling. The world needs melody not mayhem — Frank Sinatra or Shirley Bassey. I could be a Starsky and Hutch figure (although obviously there's just one of me and I'd never wear a cardigan). But just like they fight crime, I would fight to protect everyone from vile music.

'The next thing Kermit the Frog will be number one.'

'Don't be silly dear.' said mum.

'Nobody would buy a record by a puppet...'

December 6th 1976
- - - - - - - - - - - - - - - - - - - -

I woke up this morning in a cold sweat. I had another one of my weird dreams. This time I dreamt I was on that *Opportunity Knocks* and Bobby Crush was writing a song for me and I had to dress up as Orville. There's obviously something about these types of shows that give me nightmares. I think I'm going to stop watching TV forever. Anyway, the talent on there is appalling. What's wrong with television nowadays? It needs a bloody good shake up if you ask me.

December 7th 1976

There are a few spooky things that are happening to me right now. For example, I received a letter out of the blue this morning:

My dear Wizard,

I wanted you to be the first person to know. I have just been given a wild card to enter Wimbledon next year. According to the LTA, I have a very good chance of breaking into the top twenty within the next two years. So you see, Simon, you were always my inspiration. You were the first one to recognise my talent. You were the one that gave me the confidence to do this.

And now I miss you. Can we meet up pleeeease?

You are the only person in the whole world
who can help guide my career.

All my love

Valerie xx

Why the hell should I guide other people's careers?
Where's the money in that? Mind you...if I took a
percentage of her earnings I suppose it could soon
add up to quite a lot.

NOTE TO SELF:

RESEARCH THIS IDEA A BIT MORE...

December 8th 1976
— Crap music

I've been looking at the pop charts today. What a load
of crap! If they had lived 2000 years ago and sung like
that, they would have been stoned. I'm no judge; but in
my opinion, The Eagles, Rod Stewart, Elton John, Donna
Summer and Frank Sinatra have real star quality. They
all have what Mr Hammerdale called the 'X' factor.
What the world needs now is more of these *real* stars.

Last night at dinner I told mum that the music business
might well suit my many talents.

'Yes dear — but you will have to start at the bottom,'
she says.

'You just can't walk into any business and expect to be
boss.'

'Why ever not?' I said.

ME AT SCHOOL (YUK!)

'Because you have to learn the business on the way up. You might even have to start in the post room.'

'In that case I may as well have joined the bloody post office.'

As far as I'm concerned you either have talent or you don't. And I do.

December 9th 1976
— An offer I had to refuse...

Mum woke me early this morning and told me Dad wanted me in the study. I sensed trouble again. I slipped on a pair of jeans and a black John Smedley V neck and walked into the study.

To my utter horror there stood Dad and Nicholas both dressed identically in pin striped suits and wide blue ties.

'My god it's the property mafia.' I announced.

'Just pull up a chair and sit down Simon,' says dad with a straight face.

I stared at Nicholas standing with his arms folded, smirking.

'Nicholas and I have been chatting about your future,' says dad.

Nicholas nods in smug approval.

'We want to open an Estate Agency in Helstree and we think this could be a good opportunity for you,' says dad. 'We want to make you a decent offer'.

'So, Opportunity Knocks for me at last?' I said, reaching for a B&H from the silver box.

'When do I get to try on the matching suit?'

Nicholas stifles a giggle.

'Listen son,' says dad. 'You don't appear to have any

other job offers on the table and this is a good chance to learn the business and earn some money, like your brother here.'

Another nod and smirk from Nicholas.

'If I'm being honest dad I'd rather go back to school or college than join the family business. I'm just not cut out to be the property baron type.'

Dad looked resigned and reached for a Cuban from the desk drawer.

I got up to go and Nicholas caught my eye. 'You're making a big mistake,' he mutters like a line out of *The Godfather*.

'We'll see big shot. We'll see,' I said, and closed the door behind me.

My god! I'd better make sure I check my bed tonight...

December 15th 1976

— Music to my ears!

Something very weird happened this morning. I got a call out of the blue from that Pete Blackman bloke.

'Listen mate — you'll never guess what's happened.'

'What is it Pete?'

'Well, I wrote another song for Concheeta called **You Are My Hero**. Then I got her to do a demo and sent it up to EMI records. And now they want her to release it as a single?'

'No way?'

'The thing is mate. She's dumped the McDougal bloke and now she wants to talk to you.'

'Whatever for?'

'She thinks you can help her make a pop video and manage her career.'

'No way...'

'So, will you do it mate...?

So... maybe Simon's got talent after all...

25th December 1976

— Another Christmas day
— another Christmas number one.

I'm still thinking about what Pete Blackman told me. Working with Concheeta does have its appeal and it sure beats working for the Corleone family. She's one hot girl but I'm not sure whether it's the right move for me.

LET'S WEIGH IT UP:

• How much money will I make?

• Will we get a hit record?

• Is Pete just a one hit wonder?

• Does Concheeta fancy me — and do I really care?

• Am I more talented than both Concheeta *and* Pete Blackman? YES!

Well I know I've got talent; it's just a matter of which direction I want to wave my magic spells.

I spent the rest of the morning looking at brother Tony's NME. I was checking all the old Christmas number ones. Apart from Elvis and The Beatles it all makes very sad reading. Benny Hill, Jimmy Osmond, Rolf Harris, Slade and Cliff bloody Richard. Is this what the public really wants? If I'm being honest I think we need to encourage more new talent. And one quick glance at the pop charts and I'm thinking... you know what? Maybe Concheeta does have a chance.

The earth moved again.

'siiiiiiimon!'

'YES MUM?'

'Can you please get up? We're about to have brunch and Uncle Gerry and Roger Moore have just arrived and Uncle Gerry wants to talk to you about your future...'

Happy Christmas Diary!

March 5th 1977

— The day I glimpsed my future

It's 11.30pm and I'm in my bedroom writing this. I think I've just had one of those epiphany moments. I was in the bathroom looking in the mirror doing my hair — a thing I always do before going to bed — and I think I saw the future. And if I'm being honest — it was really spooky. I closed my eyes for a second and then opened them and everything was different. My face had changed, my hair was shorter, I was way taller and my teeth looked a brilliant shade of white.

And there was this fuzzy halo around my head and behind me there were people clapping me. Maybe it was a message, a realization that I had a mission to save the world.

Just like Superman.

'siiiiiimon?'

'Yes mum?

'That Pete Blackman's on the phone for you again....'

March 6th....
————————————
— Can dreams really come true...?

MY GOD I JUST WOKE UP from the dream to end all dreams...

It all appeared to be set in the future. I was about 60 years old (but looked 38) and sitting in this great big house in London. I was the Prime Minister, *and*, at the same time appearing on TV shows all over the world.

We were just about to go into rehearsals for the ninth season of *The Royals Have Talent* when I get a phone call from the Pentagon saying they are reworking the rule that you don't have to be an American citizen to be president. But I insisted I didn't *need* another big white house when I already had so many.

In the dream all my friends and family appeared to have been inspired by my incredible success. Nicholas married Dorothy Lovechop and bought a goat farm in Norfolk. Brother Tony finally read *The Stud* and wrote a book called *Hot Cornish Crumpet*, which sold six million copies. Miss Glowerbridge fell in love with Professor Fingerwood and Mr Biggers married Nanny Heather and live in the potting shed making magic potions to help sick people.

And...Concheeta went straight to number one with *You Are My Hero*.

As for mum... well, she appeared to talk throughout the whole bloody dream!

After *Bugs Have Talent* aired she was poached by American TV to replace a woman called Oprah

Winfrey and *chat with Mrs C* becomes the highest-rated talk show in America!

Just before I woke up I was having lunch with Richard Branson and we were talking about people living on the moon and how we could get TV shows up there. He was thinking ahead, and asked *me* to be the first person to have a TV show on the moon. He said it would be called *Moonstars* and then we could do *Marsstars* (no problem with the sponsor there!). He wanted to roll out the format to each and every planet in the solar system.

If I'm being honest, it's one hell of a dream. But then again, dreams can come true...can't they...?

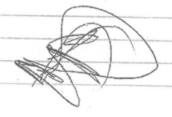